Profound and Multiple Learning Difficulties

The SEN series

Profound and Multiple Learning Difficulties

**Corinna Cartwright and
Sarah Wind-Cowie**

continuum
LONDON • NEW YORK

Continuum International Publishing Group
The Tower Building
11 York Road
London
SE1 7NX

15 East 26th Street
New York, NY 10010

British Library Cataloguing-in-Publication Data
A catalogue record for this book is available from the British Library.

ISBN: 0 8264 7836 0 (paperback)

Typeset by Servis Filmsetting Ltd, Manchester
Printed and bound in Great Britain by
MPG Books Ltd, Bodmin, Cornwall

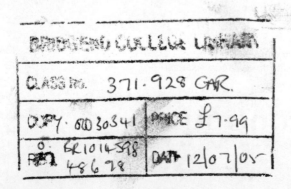

Contents

Preface

As teachers in the twenty-first century we recognize that pupils with profound and multiple learning difficulties (PMLD) not only have a right to a good education but have the ability to learn and improve their own lives and those of others. These pupils can make choices, show preferences and in some cases develop control over their environment. Through effective positioning they can focus on their environment and begin to develop meaningful relationships. In a positive educational environment pupils with PMLD can raise their self-esteem, independence and self-advocacy, qualitative opportunities that we would all take for granted.

We live in a world in which empowerment and equality are valued goals; this demands representation for those with severest needs as well as those with more moderate needs. In order for this to happen strong partnerships must be developed to ensure that multidisciplinary collaboration fosters continuity between effective programmes and daily practice.

This book aims to offer guidance for teachers and practitioners working with pupils with PMLD. The quality of the education they provide depends on their ability to keep abreast of the growing body of knowledge on teaching and learning for pupils with

PMLD, the improving communication systems being developed and the new and imaginative patterns of partnership and support.

Introduction

PMLD explained

'Profound and multiple learning difficulties' describes pupils who have profound intellectual impairment and more than one disability. These disabilities may include sensory impairments, e.g. sight and hearing loss, autism, mental illness, epilepsy, physical disabilities or debilitating medical conditions. Until 1971 these pupils were denied access to the education system being deemed uneducable. They were largely cared for in long-stay institutions where they spent their lives hidden away lying on mats and beds. Only their most basic needs were attended to.

Today we acknowledge that their needs and rights can no longer be ignored. With the advancement of medical science and techniques there are a growing number of pupils with profound and multiple learning difficulties entering schools. More premature babies are surviving, some of whom are multiply disabled. Improvements in medical science have ensured that more lives are being preserved, lives that in the past would have been lost at birth or in early childhood. The mix of pupils seen within this group is constantly changing. Over the last ten years for instance there

1

has been an enormous increase in tube-fed pupils in school.

These recent changes have influenced the numbers of agencies involved in the care and education of pupils. The growth of these specialists has been piecemeal and the numbers of experts offering advice to parents and teachers can be bewildering. It is essential for collaboration between professionals to ensure a consistent approach that meets their needs. This collaboration must include the thoughts and wishes of the parents and pupils themselves. The approach adopted must be flexible, concrete and personalized to the needs of the individual. Lastly the collaborative approach needs to identify a system or leader for meeting the needs of the individual to ensure the approach is consistently and effectively developed and shared.

Inclusion

Recently inclusion has become the overriding concern of special needs education. The concepts of integration and inclusion have become entwined and their definitions have become muddied and confused. For many inclusion is merely a matter of place, for others a political arena for human rights issues and the transference of power. Inclusion should infer an opportunity for pupils with disabilities to participate more fully in the everyday activities of modern life and benefit from the community of the school. It should also imply a quality of provision that is both beneficial to and desired by the pupil.

Relatively little research has been done to assess the value of inclusion for pupils with PMLD or even to establish what exactly it means for them. However, as teachers we should strive to provide for all pupils with PMLD the entitlement of a balanced and broadly based curriculum carried out alongside their peers when relevant and when learning objectives can be met. Pupils should have a right to self-advocacy and self-determination included in their curriculum, and as teachers we can develop this through the encouragement and fostering of choice making.

Where inclusion projects with mainstream schools take place the teachers must ask whether the provision is meeting the educational needs of the pupils as well as their integration needs. Inclusion schemes should include effective greeting activities, spontaneous interactions, cooperative group work and the opportunity to be part of a cohesive class in which the choices and the involvement of all pupils are valued. Being part of a mixed-ability class is not sufficient; communication opportunities and interactions must be taking place. The environment should not present barriers to learning; teaching quality must be maintained; activities precisely planned and the objectives for all pupils involved must be clear and achievable.

The quality of the inclusion for these pupils depends on the determination and ability of the staff involved to provide learning experiences which both meet their educational needs and encourage interactions with and the acceptance of their mainstream peers. As with other areas of their education it is dependent on the successful partnership and collaboration of all agencies concerned with their provision. Questions that the teacher should be asking when establishing an inclusion programme may include:

- Is the accommodation suitable? Are there disabled toilet facilities? Is there wheelchair access to all necessary areas? Are play areas suitable? Are there quiet areas that can be used following a seizure?

- Are there opportunities for joint planning to ensure relevant objectives and activities for all pupils?

- What equipment may be needed to ensure continuity of provision?

- How will group work be developed?

- How will physical programmes be incorporated in the sessions?

- Is there any preparatory work necessary with the mainstream pupils?

- How will interactions be developed?

- Does there need to be any staff training or joint staff discussion between schools?

- How will the programme be monitored?

- How will the assessment of the programme feed back to the Senior Management Team and Governors?

1

The Daily Management of Pupils with PMLD

In establishing education programmes for pupils with PMLD their personal needs and physical management cannot be ignored. Consideration for daily living skills and general mobility is essential, not as separate programmes developed apart from the general curriculum but as an integral part of school life. The key to developing programmes lies in the ability of the teacher to recognize the pupil's personal desires and motivations and to combine it with a collaborative approach with other key professionals. Such programmes should concentrate on facilitating independence, transferring control and establishing communication.

Issues of physical management can give teachers concern and where possible the development of individualized management programmes for their needs should be established. Some of the most common areas for physical management and questions requiring answers are listed below.

Position and mobility

The physical management of pupils with PMLD appears complex but the development of a clear dual strategy for postural care and the maintenance of function is essential. A collaborative multidisciplinary approach must be established and implemented and shared by all those involved in the care of the pupil. This should include the parents as principal carers. Carers should be at the centre of discussions, and other agencies should see themselves in a facilitating role.

When the human body has difficulty in moving in the usual symmetrical way there is a tendency for it to become fixed in asymmetric shapes. It is essential that all carers understand the need for a consistent approach to postural care. In encouraging function the prime consideration should be to encourage independence. Effective functional programmes for pupils with cerebral palsy are those which become part of the pupil's daily life where aims are long-term rather than short-term.

Over the years a range of specific therapeutic approaches to posture and mobility have been developed such as Conductive Education developed in Hungary by Andras Peto, the Bobath approach developed at the Western Cerebral Palsy Centre, the Patterning approach developed at the Brainwave Centre or the MOVE approach developed in the USA. Comparative studies of all the approaches indicate that although many sound intentions and principles are demonstrated they can have some shortcomings. It is undoubtedly the case that when pupils are given access to intensive and prolonged courses of physiotherapy they are likely to demonstrate improvement. Some of these therapeutic approaches have provided us with sound and valuable advice, e.g. Bobath on the development of postural and functional programmes.

Bobath encourages an emphasis on working with parents and pupils from an early age to prevent the formation of deformities and develop skilled movement for everyday life and self-help activities. The main aim of the Bobath method is to facilitate movement by inhibiting tonic reflex activity associated with abnormal posture and abnormal movement patterns and through the development of more mature postural reflexes. The physiotherapist will recommend the use of normal patterns of muscle actions, such as lifting of the head, rolling over from back to tummy, sitting up, the development of balance and righting reflexes through the use of positions in which they can achieve these movements. This is combined with the development of the unconscious functioning self through an encouragement to feel textures, shapes and temperatures. Basic sensory motor activities are learning experiences and should ensure that therapy and education become integrated.

In choosing a course of action it is important to get the balance right. To base practice on short-term functional goals with little consideration for long-term care or to attend so rigidly to postural considerations that function is lost are both short-sighted options. Skilled handling of cerebral palsy pupils requires programmes of physiotherapy that are incorporated into the general pattern of daily living and the school curriculum.

Programmes should be appropriate to the pupil's level of health and capability but also encourage independence and useful function. The physical programmes should be developed by a team including a physiotherapist, parents, a teacher or carer and where possible an occupational therapist. The programmes should be used by all the agencies concerned and eventually become part of the pattern for daily living.

Careful counselling of parents will ensure that

parents are protected from a plethora of new theories that appeal to susceptible parents eager for instant and dramatic improvements.

The provision of specialist equipment for positioning and mobility can assist physical function, minimize abnormal reflexes and reactions, prevent contractures and facilitate independence.

Epilepsy

Epilepsy can be a distressing condition for the pupil and those who care for the pupil. This distress can be minimized through appropriate care for the pupil, guidance for parents and training for the staff.

One in 133 people in the UK has epilepsy – around 440,000. This makes it the second most common neurological condition after migraine. In the past those with epilepsy faced stigma and prejudice. These attitudes are changing, though there are still those who try to limit the opportunities in life of those with epilepsy through fear or lack of knowledge. Epilepsy today can usually be controlled with the correct medical treatment.

A seizure is caused by a temporary change in the way brain cells work. The brain consists of a vast network of nerve cells called neurons. Millions of electrical messages are fired between these cells, controlling every single thing we think, feel or do. However, sometimes a disturbance in brain chemistry causes the signals to alter. When this happens the neurons fire off faster than usual and in erratic bursts leading to a seizure or fit. During a seizure pupils may black out, collapse or experience a number of unusual sensations or movements. The seizure usually only lasts a matter of seconds or minutes, after which the brain cells return to normal.

The staff in the class should keep a clear record of seizures and information should also be kept available about the nature and care of the individual pupil with epilepsy. It is essential for any practitioner working with the pupil to be aware of the following information.

Epilepsy History and Guidelines	
Pupil's name:	Date:
Cause of epilepsy	
Regularity of seizures	
Form of seizures	
Pattern and frequency	
Warning signs and triggers	
Medical attention required	
Drugs administered, timing advice, repeat administration	
Emergency actions	
Actions and care	
Effects and side-effects of drugs administered	
Additional protection necessary, e.g. helmet	
Risk assessments	
Staff training necessary	
Learning needs of the pupil	
Professional guidance Telephone:	

Profound and Multiple Learning Difficulties

Specimen Seizure Chart	
Name of pupil:	
Routines to be followed in the event of a seizure	
Medication to be given, dosage and timings	
Signature and date	

All staff should be aware of routines and procedures regarding seizures:

◆ Ensure the pupil is not at risk of injury from his/her environment.

◆ If the pupil is mobile, place pupil in recovery position. If the child is in a wheelchair, leave but observe to ensure the airway stays open. Some pupils have suction that can be used after the seizure. In these cases it should only be used following training from a nurse or doctor.

◆ Time the seizure and follow medication and emergency procedures as laid down in medical guidelines. If in a public place carry a small blanket or coat that can be used to cover the pupil if rectal medication is to be given.

◆ Ensure privacy is maintained as far as is reasonably possible.

◆ Ensure pupils who regularly witness seizures are told about procedures and how they might help, e.g. calling another adult.

The Daily Management of Pupils with PMLD

Record of Seizures					
Date	Time	Length of seizure	Description and action taken	Persons notified	Signature

♦ Ensure parents are aware of seizures that occur.

♦ Ensure seizures are recorded and charts made available for medicals and reviews (see Specimen Seizure Chart).

Continence

A well-managed programme for continence helps to ensure a reduced risk of skin problems and infections, improved physical comfort and increased self-esteem. Although in some cases incontinence cannot be cured it can be well-managed. Effective management of continence can mean transferring a negative and stigmatized issue into part of a positive daily living pattern.

There are many misconceptions about continence and these must be eradicated if an effective regime for continence is to be established. It should be remembered that achieving continence does not require a high level of intellectual function and can be achieved for many through routine and training. Liquid intake should not be reduced as this will lead to an increased risk of infections. Pupils should be taken to the toilet every two to three hours to establish a normal urinary cycle and only be taken half-hourly if it is part of a short-term training programme.

If instigating a regime to establish continence, it is worth securing guidance from a continence adviser. Accurate assessment and diagnosis is crucial for successful treatment. Once a routine is established, ensure all practitioners and carers involved follow the same routine. This will help the pupil understand the

Name of pupuil:	
Continence Information	
Nature of continence needs	
Times of continence routine	
Order for established routine including the order of clothes removed	
Words, songs used during the routine	

process and anticipate what will happen next. The following chart may be useful.

For those for whom continence is not a possibility routine, comfort and privacy must be consistent. As so many more pupils are now in co-located schools and in mainstream environments sensitivity to the issues of confidentiality and privacy is even more poignant. Staff involved in toileting programmes should be trained in appropriate moving and handling guidelines and be aware of routines and procedures for the individual pupil.

Diet

Diet is an important area of daily living both as a means of survival and as a pleasurable experience. It also provides us with a powerful opportunity for choice-making, something we take for granted but which enables the pupil with PMLD to anticipate, initiate and ultimately control situations. In developing a programme for eating and drinking the teacher should consider the following:

♦ Mealtimes are occasions that should be developed collaboratively using advice from speech therapists, occupational therapists, physiotherapists and dieticians. Many schools now see mealtimes for pupils as part of the learning day and feeding programmes are seen as educational programmes included in the hours recorded as curriculum time. Attention should be given to choice-making, anticipation, likes and dislikes and signals used to demonstrate these responses. These times need to be carefully developed, planned, monitored and where appropriate recorded.

♦ Ensure the methods used at home have been explored. Parents feed their children every day and have often developed techniques that enable the pupil to feel at ease and confident. The same methods should be applied to all mealtime situations. Where inappropriate methods are used at home some support and guidance may be necessary and the provision made for useful equipment.

♦ Ensure that mealtimes are relaxed, not rushed and provide opportunities for communication. Rushing at mealtimes can mean that potent opportunities for developing independence and fine motor skills are lost. If a child can hold a spoon but not direct it make sure staff give only sufficient support to enable the pupil to eat and not remove the independence that has already been developed.

◆ Pupils with cerebral palsy often find it easier and an aid to digestion to eat in a stander.

◆ Some pupils may require specialist cutlery and crockery. Speech therapists can provide guidance on using cutlery and cups and techniques to aid chewing and swallowing and prevention of the bite and gag reflex. The use of a small spoon in the early stages will encourage the pupil to take food using the upper lip. The correct positioning of the hand on the lower jaw provides support and aids control. Facial programmes to ensure correct muscle function may be necessary prior to eating in order to assist pupils' facial muscular control. These programmes should be developed by the speech therapist with all the carers concerned.

◆ Establish a routine for eating that all practitioners are aware of, including knowledge of quantities normally consumed, favourite foods and preferred textures, techniques used, waiting time, signals for likes, dislikes and the desire to pause. Where necessary establish a training programme for staff concerned.

◆ Regular weight recording and dietary programmes that effect weight management should be established for obese pupils, normal weight control and for underweight pupils. This should be balanced with as flexible a dietary regime as possible to allow for choice-making and pleasure.

♦ Ensure that the diet is balanced, providing sufficient fibre, fluids, vitamins and minerals. Pupils who have obsessional disorders may not take in sufficient variety to maintain adequate nutrition. In these cases nutritional supplements may be necessary.

♦ Where pupils are tube-fed advice from a nurse should be sought.

♦ Independence skills may be developed through switch programmes, e.g. by allowing a pupil to mix a shake using a food processor and switching system.

Bearing these considerations in mind ensure that the staff give the pupil time to make his/her own choices and demonstrate preferences. Reinforcement of communication should be as important at mealtimes as during educational programmes. Food can be a powerful motivator for pupils with PMLD and a useful time for the development of communication skills and self-advocacy.

For some pupils mealtimes can be stressful, resulting in abnormal reflexes and disrupted patterns of movement. For these pupils a quiet environment away from the bustle of the canteen may be preferable. Here likes, dislikes and new experiences in texture and tastes can be explored in relaxed surroundings away from the pressures of time.

2

Learning Environments

In order to unlock the learning potential of pupils with profound and multiple learning difficulties it is essential to begin with the environment in which learning takes place. It must be an environment in which the pupil feels safe and in which interaction can occur spontaneously. In order for this to happen the pupil must be able to make sense of the space in which learning occurs. For pupils with sensory impairments the everyday environment can be unpredictable and confusing. The visual and spoken markers that we take for granted are not acknowledged, established conventions not recognized and the spoken experiences of others not absorbed. It is therefore necessary to adapt the space to shut out distant sensory clutter and allow the pupil to focus on the immediate environment. This local environment of places and objects must be combined with a social environment of interactive and caring people. In such an environment a pupil with PMLD can become an active and communicative person and begin to recognize their own capacity for control. Lastly the pupil needs to be given time to become aware, pay attention to, anticipate and begin to control an environment in which he/she is learning.

The physical environment

The physical space

In creating suitable environments for pupils with PMLD the assumption that this must be away from their peers, in specially designed rooms with a range of high-tech equipment is outdated. Sensory Rooms are undoubtedly one type of environment that fosters learning in pupils with PMLD but few believe today that the model of 'special care' provision is desirable. Pupils with PMLD are increasingly being included in groups with their age peers, whether in a special or main-stream school. In an increasing number of areas pupils with PMLD are now leaving school and attending colleges alongside their peer group.

Sensory impairment of one form or another is present in 80 per cent of pupils with PMLD. It is essential that this is acknowledged when considering the physical environment.

♦ Pupils with hearing loss will find it difficult to concentrate if noisy fans or heaters are present or where there is the distant sound of clattering from the kitchen. Padded screens, false ceilings, wall hangings and thick carpets all help to cut out additional sounds. Hearing aids, headphones, and radio mike loops help to heighten auditory experience.

♦ Standard strip lighting tends to produce a light that allows poor demarcation between surfaces for those with visual impairments. Areas within a room or space can be more clearly demarcated with lamps, spots, overhead lights with a range of coloured bulbs or by the absence of light. Through the use of textures, objects of reference and scents staff can be recognized by those with visual loss.

♦ Temperature and humidity must also be taken into account. Rooms adapted for sensory work are often airless, stuffy and poorly ventilated. Although warm environments are necessary for pupils with PMLD the temperature must be controlled and access to fresh air is essential.

Sensory spaces

Pupils with PMLD may have fragmented learning patterns in which achievement is slow and based on sensory experience and simple perceptions. The sensory space may be one of the few environments available to the individual with PMLD where he/she is able to function at a near independent level. In breaking down these barriers to learning we can provide an important bridge to inclusion. When pupils can function with some independence and have fun they are also more likely to interact socially. Maintaining a simple chart to record the most important preferences for daily living and sensory learning can be a good starting point for the sensory room.

Sensory spaces should be shaped by the needs of the individual users and the imagination and sensitivity of the staff using them. More equipment does not necessarily mean improved provision. Likewise expensive does not mean more success. Often cheap home-made items can be equally successful.

Sensory curriculum techniques are constantly being

Profound and Multiple Learning Difficulties

Student summary for planning
Name: Date:
Communication methods used:
Visual factors to be considered:
Auditory factors to be considered:
Physical factors to be considered:
Best type of switch:
Ideal switch position:
Position favoured for work:
Position favoured for relaxing:
Physiotherapy required to facilitate work:
Favourite items:
Favourite music:
Key workers:
Favourite peers:
Proximity to speaker required:
Favourite tactile experience:
Favourite visual experience:
Best time of day for work:
Best time of day to relax:
Medical considerations:

Tastes and textures:
Feeding:
Smells:
Symbol/pictoral considerations:
P Scale achieved:
Long-term aim:
Strategies:
Short-term aim:
Strategies:
Communicative signals:
Equipment needed for: Vision:
Hearing:
Touch:
Taste:
Smell:
Movement:

defined and redefined. Recently the change towards personalized learning through the understanding of preferred learning styles and the development of Intensive Social Interaction techniques have changed the way in which we use sensory spaces. When developing programmes the adult should sensitively guide the pupil towards the next stage of play or interaction. The pupil should recognize their place in initiating an action rather than being part of an adult-led activity. The combination of physical and social emphases on the learning has also shaped recent approaches to sensory spaces. It is not merely the contents of the room that matter but the ability of the teacher to use the room effectively to meet the needs of the individual pupil.

The sensory curriculum should incorporate clear objectives for learning developed through interaction and feedback. The sensory space should also encourage the process of discovery, independence, pupil-led experiences, choice-making and time for relaxation. It should not be a place where you provide an alternative curriculum but a place where you enable pupils to have access to an inclusive curriculum.

A baseline of sensory achievement should be established before beginning programmes.

Real-life experiences

There is no replacement for real-life experiences. Educational trips are a vital element of the curriculum so that pupils can experience the hustle and bustle of the high street, a supermarket, traffic and changing weather patterns. Parents can be reluctant to take their children out with them and their everyday experiences of life become impoverished. By collecting items and photographs to revisit the trip once back in school the pupil can begin to develop memories and the potential for imagination.

Within the classroom the materials pupils interact with should not merely be plastic toys but a range of sensory-rich everyday articles: bunches of keys, scrubbing brushes, hot-water bottles, spoons, scourers, dusters, saucepans, shoelaces. The materials should encourage experience through touch, smell, taste and sound, sight and movement. The materials should provide endless exploratory opportunities of touching, mouthing, sucking, scratching, stretching, sniffing, filling, emptying, tapping, banging and stroking, etc., depending on the level of development that the pupil is at. The adult should be attentive, giving the pupil every opportunity for interaction and exploration but allowing the pupil maximum potential for unlocking his/her curiosity and self-motivation.

Ultraviolet light

An ultraviolet light environment provides an effective backdrop for learning for pupils with profound and multiple learning difficulties. Under ultraviolet light fluorescent colours become thirty times as bright as colours under ordinary light and thus encourage exploration and focused attention. The clarity aids visual understanding and gives a heightened awareness of space and movement.

There are some health and safety issues that should be acknowledged. Ultraviolet light is one part of the electromagnetic spectrum, which also includes, infrared radiation, X-rays, visible light and microwaves, radiowaves. Radiation has different effects on the body depending on its wavelength. Ultraviolet radiation is invisible and lies just beyond the violet end of the visible light spectrum. The lamps used in dark rooms, multisensory rooms and black boxes emit ultraviolet radiation. UVR is divided into three regions which all have different effects on the body.

♦ UVC radiation – has little penetrating power but can cause burns to skin and eyes. It is never used in dark rooms.

♦ UVB radiation – used in sunlamps and can cause harm to eyes and skin. It is never used in dark rooms.

♦ UVA radiation – much less damaging and very rarely harms eyes and skin. A very few members of the population are sensitive. UVA radiation is used in dark rooms

Risk assessments should note the following recommended exposure limits:

Children   five hours per day
Adults   one hour per day.

Where pupils are on medication it would be wise to check with the doctor about the specific guidance before planning a programme in an ultraviolet light area. Some drugs have specific reactions so staff should avoid use of ultraviolet light with individuals using tranquillizers and antibiotics. Bergamot oils can increase photosensitivity and should not be used in ultraviolet light areas. If a member of staff has any doubts about its use it is wise to consult the pupil's paediatrician.

Specimen programmes for ultraviolet light

The object of this next activity would be for the pupil to develop awareness and begin to attend to the events around him/her. Through the reactions of the pupil the observer can begin to distinguish preferences.

The play patterns established during the following programme should be initiated by the child him/herself who chooses what to play and how to play it.

Personalized spaces

Small spaces or corners can be personalized for a pupil. Interactive Boxes or Little Rooms (open-ended perspex boxes designed by Lilli Neilson) are controlled environments that provide pupils with the ingredients for moving on. Pupils at the earliest stages of development may need hanging bunches of keys, bangles, beads and chains to brush against or furry and rough textures to encounter through tiny hand or leg movements. The movement of the items provides auditory, tactile and visual feedback. Tactile-defensive pupils may prefer to explore with their feet. These environments provide secure spaces in which to encourage active exploration.

Those pupils developing an understanding of cause and effect may include switches operating fans and CD players. Be creative with your layout to encourage movement, e.g. rolling to press switches for a pupil with cerebral palsy. Do not be tempted to constantly move things. Pupils will learn where things are and through constant repetition develop a sense of object permanence. Through the pupil's growing awareness he/she learns to initiate exploration in the surrounding environment and develop intentionality.

Profound and Multiple Learning Difficulties

Programme for P1/P2 (i)				
Name .... Date				
Programme objective: *This should reflect the personalized learning programme or the Individual Education Plan of the pupil concerned.*				
Activity	Stimulus	Attention/ eye contact/ timescale	Expression/ animation/ movement	Inter-actions
UV Light programme	Hanging CDs painted with fluorescent paint or paper plates on stick with fluorescent faces. Track faces as they move slowly from side to side and up and down. Fluorescent face-paint or sunblock on own faces, use of mirror to view. Both pupil and adult need to be painted. Use of spectacles painted with fluorescent paint.			
	Fluorescent ribbons tied to chair, child or to a structure around the pupil. Use of hair dryer. Make ribbons flutter.			
	Fluorescent mittens or gloves on pupil's own hands. Tubing should be hanging around the pupil's head, hands filled with fluorescent paint. Ensure the tubing is close enough to brush and touch.			

Programme for P2 (ii) and P3 (ii)				
Name .... Date				
Programme objective: *This should reflect the personalized learning programme or the Individual Education Plan of the pupil concerned.*				
Activity	Media	Attention/ eye contact/ movement	Reaching, grasping and anticipating	Inter- actions
UV Light programme	Using papier mâché eggs covered with fluorescent paint in a tray encourage exploration and handling.			
	Explore fluorescent paint in a tray with added cornflour.			
	Fluorescent ping-pong balls and Koosh balls can be hung on string around a pupil to enable reaching and grasping.			
	Use white gloves to encourage eye contact with hand movements.			
	Commercially made and home-made magic rods and wands in different colours in a tray to explore handle and look at.			
	Paint fluorescent paint on home-made yoghurt-pot shakers with rice, beans, paper-clips, etc., inside. Provide a range to explore.			
	White velcro and a black velcro board with fluorescent material shapes as an optional extra.			

The social environment

People are the most important aspect of the pupil's environment. The balance between providing support and opportunities for independence and the development of learned passivity and dependence is a delicate one. Good relationships are essential to enable the development of trust. The growth of trust provides a security through which pupils develop an increased self-awareness and self-esteem, the essential background for learning. The following are pointers for good working relationships with pupils with profound and multiple learning difficulties.

♦ Get to know the pupil, their likes and dislikes, capabilities – physical and communicative, their preferred learning styles, their signals and their preferred learning environments. You must be able to see the world through the eyes of the learner, not just what they see, but how they see it. The adult should be aware of preferences for sound, temperature, touch and speed and be able to recognize when the time is right to withdraw support. Ensure all agencies working with the pupil have a shared understanding and have a central document to which they can refer.

♦ Allow the pupil to direct his/her environment in all activities. React to what the pupil offers, building it into a communicative exchange. Do not continually focus on talking to or at the learner, naming objects, commenting on the learner's movements and activities. Instead try to participate in the pupil's learning experiences. Talking too much may result in interfering in the focus of the learner's interest. Constant questioning and control will lead to withdrawal and learned passivity. Look for cues from the learner and try to ensure stimulation is active rather than passive.

♦ Where activities are passive ensure that the routines stay the same to enable anticipation, e.g. care activities such as washing and changing; a pupil who knows the routines for using cold wet wipes or tissues for nose blowing will anticipate actions and react appropriately.

♦ Be keenly observant. Record all significant observations. Signals may be unconventional. The child's self-expression may be for their own gratification rather than as a means of communication. The observer has to show that he/she has understood the signal and through his/her responses enable the pupil to become a participant in their interactions. Your actions show the pupil that what she/he does has meaning. Inward signals of self-expression must become outward signals for a communicating world. Gradually the pupil begins to recognize that a shared meaning exists. If a mismatch in this interaction process occurs the pupil is likely to give up and withdraw into his/her own world.

♦ Give the pupil plenty of time. It takes the learner with profound and multiple learning difficulties longer to process information, and to organize a response. Wait time needs to be built into every programme. This will allow the pupil to gain confidence and recognize their own capacity to influence what happens next. Repetition of the same sensory programmes for long enough will allow anticipation and recognition. This may take months of work.

♦ Do not be tempted to make things happen as this will lead to domination of the pupil and withdrawal from interactions. Those with physical disabilities will need to be taught some skills coactively; working interactively with the pupil the adult should always allow the pupil to take the lead. Recognizing signals, learning his/her preferences and guiding without leading are skills that take time to develop for each pupil. Knowing when to withdraw is an essential skill.

♦ Recognize when the pupil has worked for long enough. Negative responses should be as valued as positive ones. They are both successful achievements in communication.

♦ Concentrate on what the pupil does well. Weaknesses should not be ignored but learners should be seen primarily for what they can do. The learner cannot hope to take the lead in his/her education if all the objectives have not yet been realized. Building on success develops confidence and motivation.

♦ Value the learner's perspective and do not be tempted to impose your own personality on that of the learner. Respond to the pupil by reflecting back what the pupil is doing, in the same mood and volume.

♦ Ensure interactions are not confined to work programmes but are part of all daily routines. Apply the same principles for work in all settings.

♦ Try not to compartmentalize learning opportunities. The P levels are generic for levels 1–3 and therefore the adult working with the pupil should see the 'subject' as merely a context in which the next small steps of a pupil can be realized. Emphasis on a discrete subject can become too strictly focused on specific skills enhancement and a timetabled subject becomes an end in itself. Pupils with PMLD need to have flexibility built into their programmes to enable adults to capitalize on events and interactions that may occur.

♦ Careful attention to group work is important. The adult must consider the size of the group, the position with regards to any sensory impairment that may be present, the time required for each child to respond and the preferred learning styles of individuals in the group. Although pupils working in groups often work in parallel rather than together it is possible to build activities that encourage awareness of one another and some simple social interactions, e.g. through singing songs which foster an atmosphere of fun and community.

♦ Evaluate your work and your own interactions as well as those of the pupil. Realizing what you did well and badly will help you work better in the future.

We hear much about the importance of Assessment for Learning today. This guidance is consistent with the principles of Assessment for Learning.

Assessment for Learning reflects a significant shift from a position in which the professionals have power over the individual pupil to one in which there is a shared control of opportunities and decisions. Using Assessment for Learning as a tool enables the process of assessing, learning and moving forwards to become inseparable.

3

Teaching and Learning

This chapter lays down a model for working with pupils with PMLD. It also takes a new look at the way we plan and a means of interpreting and implementing what is a weighty and potentially cumbersome curriculum. Some guidance as to the way in which practitioners should develop good working relationships with pupils with PMLD has been provided in the previous chapter and should be used in conjunction with the following working practices.

Most teachers of pupils with PMLD use a range of approaches to promote learning which include behaviourist and cognitive models which today are not seen as mutually exclusive. A pupil's action interferes with the pattern of events and requires a modification of the social or physical environment. Adjustments occur and if consistently repeated a strategy is learned. Each experience is shaped by previous ones. Experiences in the future must be linked to those of the past if the activities are to be of value.

As pupils with PMLD are instrumental in developing their own strategies and learning pathways, a linear or highly prescriptive curriculum will lead to disjointed and unconnected learning. In establishing a curriculum it is important to realize that learning experiences must be appropriate to the child's needs and only the context for learning should change. This is reflected by the development of P1–3 of the P scales which are generic for all subjects. Individual Education Plans will reflect the level of interaction and the targets will then be applicable in a range of contexts or curricular areas.

Routine and choice

Routine enables the pupil to make sense of what is happening, to anticipate events, develop learned responses and initiate actions. An established routine cuts out confusion and gives pupils the opportunities for control. Movement between activities and fixed daily routines happens as a matter of course but possibly with little thought for those to whom the process can be bewildering. Flexibility must not be jeopardized in the classroom, but it should be combined with clear points of reference which are known to the pupil with PMLD. Routine should not limit choice but instead build it into the daily schedule through:

♦ Visual timetables. These must incorporate opportunities for choice of activity and choice of rewards.

♦ Established sequences for daily activities such as registration, toileting, hand washing, feeding, etc., should be built on the preferences of the pupil.

♦ Set sequences for anticipating change such as an established song, an object of reference or a symbol will enable the pupil to learn that the unexpected can and does happen without distress.

Planning

Personalized learning involves changing the way we think about planning and re-evaluating our roles in the education of pupils with PMLD and the organization of the school. Pupil-centred planning ensures a move towards inclusion and an improvement in the quality of life as perceived by the individual pupil. The recent document *Removing the Barriers to Learning* (DfES 2004) says:

> We are actively exploring how to make education more responsive to individual children – how to deliver personalised learning. This means:
>
> ♦ Having high expectations of all children
> ♦ Building on the knowledge and interests of every child
> ♦ Involving children in their own learning through shared objectives and feedback (assessment for learning)
> ♦ Helping children to become confident learners
> ♦ Enabling children to develop the skills they will need beyond school.

Adrian is a young man with cerebral palsy who will not learn to read, write or involve himself in mathematical calculations but he loves to socialize and communicate to be part of his peer group, laugh when they laugh and be sad when they are sad. Pupils like Adrian should be given opportunities to choose their own lifestyle.

Questions should be asked such as:

'What can we do better to improve his life now and for the future?'

In order to answer the question the teacher must know him well: who he is, what he likes and dislikes, what makes him tick, what is important to him and what he appears to want from his life.

'All about me files'

These files aim to develop a pupil-centred planning approach. There are no hard and fast rules about pupil-centred planning. In fact it invites us to look at pupil learning in a variety of ways and ensure that planning meets the needs of the pupils, not the needs of managers. Planning should be focused on what the pupil can do and likes to do using terminology that is appropriate for everyone, not just the staff.

Sections in a Pupil-Centred Plan may include:

Essential information

♦ Medical, including drugs and their side-effects

♦ Physiotherapy – movement and position

♦ Use of cutlery and cups

♦ Communication – notes about preferred learning styles and methodology

♦ Dietary guidance

♦ Social – what makes the pupil happy or unhappy

♦ Family notes

♦ Handling routines

♦ Toileting guidelines

♦ Individual Education Plans

♦ Pupil Statement

Profound and Multiple Learning Difficulties

Important information

♦ Prefers a cool environment

♦ Environment – calm or robust play

♦ Bath time is a favourite time of day

♦ Hydrotherapy relaxes

♦ Minibus rides excite

♦ Wind machines are wonderful

♦ Attention should be undivided

♦ Food should not be mashed

Enjoys/prefers/dislikes

♦ Likes people who are bubbly and energetic but not loud

♦ Hates having hair brushed

♦ Loathes parsnips

♦ Loves milk shakes

♦ Prefers gravy on greens not potatoes

The plan should then include programmes and assessment procedures. Wherever possible this should be seen as the property of the individual pupil to ensure it grows and changes as they do. This is not just a new set of paperwork, it is a move towards supporting and including the pupil's own views and perspective within the community and curriculum of the school.

Medium Term Planning should be inclusive wherever possible but take account of the pupil-centred planning findings established in the 'All about me file'. Programmes should not change weekly but be established for half-term blocks to ensure the development of attention and anticipation. Short-term planning should take account of the findings of previous sessions and allow them to inform the way in which the next session unfolds.

Assessment

Assessment can be broken down into Assessment *for* Learning and Assessment *of* Learning.

♦ Assessment for Learning should happen all the time as a part of good classroom practice. Assessment for Learning shares learning objectives with pupils, provides feedback which identifies strengths and areas for development, involves pupils in self-assessment and has a commitment that every pupil can improve. It is a formative assessment.

♦ Assessment of Learning is carried out at the end of a unit of work, term, year, key stage or when a pupil leaves or starts at a new school. It provides judgements about a pupil's level of performance in relation to National Standards – Levels. It is a sumative assessment.

Assessment for Learning should be embedded in everyday classroom practice. Teachers are increasingly recognizing the need to allow pupils to take the lead in their learning process and ensure daily learning informs future learning. This is as relevant for pupils with PMLD as anyone else. For more information on this see the section 'The social environment' (Chapter 2, pp. 27–31). In the next two sections we look at summative assessment and affective communication assessment.

Summative Assessment

Pupils in mainstream schools have been working on nationally agreed targets in order to measure performance for many years now. Special schools had no statutory benchmarks and had to be zero-rated until the publication of *Supporting the Target Setting Process* in 1998. As a result the process of summative assessment in special schools has now changed. As from 2001 special schools are also required to create targets and move towards the Government's Five-Stage Cycle for School Improvement. The QCA provided P Scales to assist with this for all pupils working below Level 1 of the National Curriculum. The P Scales are an inclusive system for assessment that dovetail into the National Curriculum Levels.

P1– P3 are generic levels that are appropriate across the curriculum. They cover the ability levels of pupils seen as operating at a profound level. Pupils move slowly through these levels. The breadth of experience and transference of skills to new contexts is seen as crucial within the assessment process at P1–P3. The development of a range of commercial systems for small steps such as PIVATs or B Squared help to provide teachers with a system for assessment that allows all pupils the opportunities for yearly progression. These systems and the P Scales allow special schools to take part in the collection of data to inform target setting at a whole school, cohort, year group and IEP level. They have allowed special schools to be part of the inclusive process of producing National Curriculum Levels for all pupils.

Affective Communication Assessment

In normal early child development parents and carers respond to the expressions and utterances of the child as if it has meaning long before the child actually begins to formulate coherent speech. The child's communication is pre-intentional in that it is given meaning by the receiver of the communication and not the instigator of it. If the adult responses are consistent, a move towards intentional communication develops as the child realizes it can achieve its goal through repeating the sound or expression.

The PMLD child has many barriers to developing intentionality since they may lack many of the behaviours that parents and carers intuitively respond to. If the child cannot or will not make good eye contact, if there are physical disabilities that make gesturing impossible or uncontrollable, if they have a visual or hearing impairment, these will affect the ability to behave in a manner perceived as being communicative and without this perception the child will not get the consistent responses needed to allow them to move to the next stage of communication.

The Affective Communication Assessment was developed by Coupe *et al.* (1988) to enable those working with PMLD students to identify positive and negative responses to a range of stimuli, and from those responses to build a 'vocabulary' for the student.

The first part of the assessment is to identify a range of stimuli that the student is known to respond to in some way. Stimuli should cover as many of the senses as possible, including tastes, smells, sounds and textures. A chart is provided which gives the means to record both movement and vocalization and any changes in the rate of these. The stimuli are introduced one by one, in small amounts, and not only the effect recorded but also the observers' interpretation of what the student felt about the stimuli. Short sessions over a number of weeks may be held and then the recording sheets are examined with the aim of identifying behaviours that are consistently associated with the observers' interpretations.

The second part of the assessment is to test the behaviours that have been identified. If the observers propose that the student claps and vocalizes when communicating that they like something they have to use a new set of stimuli to see if this continues to be the case.

A successful outcome of the assessment would be that communications for a small range of meanings would be established for the student and through rewarding them with the desired outcome each time the communication was observed the student would begin to connect their communication with the outcome of it and move towards intentionality.

There are many factors that can make the accurate collection of this kind of data difficult with the PMLD student. The health and comfort of the student, the environment, the time of day all may vary and affect results or the student may only clearly react to those stimuli they do not like, or vice versa. Sessions are ideally videotaped to allow plenty of time for adults to look at and discuss their interpretations and, if not videoed, need at least two staff to administer and observe. These things aside it is a good model for working closely with the student and for using what they can give to you to improve their communicative power and therefore the control they can exert on their lives.

4

The Curriculum

Today the curriculum for pupils with profound and multiple learning difficulties must be guided by the statutory requirements and modified according to the needs of the pupils as assessed by those who work with them. This can include a wide group of professionals, parents and carers. The curriculum is the vehicle through which a child learns and as such must be appropriate, broadly based, include statutory requirements, take note of key skills, physical and medical considerations, communication systems and acknowledge developmental aims.

This is a daunting challenge to a teacher who may feel that subject-specific concepts, skills and knowledge may not be attainable. An imaginative teacher will find subject-specific contexts to broaden experiences while developing progress towards generic targets. As an example a regular educational visit to town with the class may help a pupil understand that the world exists beyond the home and class and thus be the foundation of geographical concepts.

Teachers need to look for ways in which the different demands of the curriculum can be effectively overlapped and worked in partnership with each other. The roles of education, therapy and care must be precisely defined and then thoughtfully integrated. It is important therefore that all members of the multidisciplinary team share the goals and strategies involved in a pupil's education programmes. The balance of processes for particular pupils will vary according to a range of individual factors.

The quality of education for pupils with PMLD depends on the capabilities of the professionals involved in their learning. No two pupils with PMLD are the same and therefore the success of the approach used will depend on the teacher's capacity for flexibility, collaboration with professionals, integrated approaches and his/her success at understanding and interpreting the pupil's needs. Recently the growing number of publications which exemplify good practice and improved Internet access to information have helped staff keep abreast of new perspectives on appropriate curriculums and working techniques for pupils with PMLD.

Literacy

The National Literacy Strategy is designed to provide a practical structure for the delivery of literacy. By literacy the National Literacy Strategy has emphasized the use of literature to develop reading and writing. For pupils with PMLD the access to literacy is through the development of communication skills which are generic to all subjects at levels P1–P3 of the P Scales. Literature can provide contexts for the development of communication skills. Early writing and reading skills may be met through a range of sensory activities and books in a variety of stimulating and exciting ways. More recently, there has been recognition of the speaking and listening strand of the National Curriculum. The following section aims to help develop relevant and appropriate programmes for reading, writing and communication through intensive social interaction.

Reading

Stories should be interactive

Pupils with PMLD should be given the opportunity to become part of the story and influence the storyline. There are a wide range of high-tech resources that can be used to enable this to take place, but also a range of everyday sensory objects that can be equally effective. The following are examples of interactive stories. The objectives need to be clearly established for each pupil before embarking on the programme and these will influence the way in which you proceed with the story.

In telling a story about pirates the wind and spray are simulated with huge fans and water sprays. Repetition is encouraged through the use of 'yes' or 'more' on a Big Mack switch. Pupils hold ropes and gaze through sails flapped above their heads. Warm sand and shells are felt as the pirates climb up the beach and cool water is provided when symbols are exchanged. The pupils make choices of treasures from a box full of tinsel, baubles and silver foil. They gaze at themselves in a mirror. Patches and scars are painted on their faces. Time to head back to sea with the sail and spray. Following a sea shanty song and a warm drink we head back to class.

Example Sensory Big Book – **Where the Forest Meets the Sea** *by Jeannie Baker*

A group of ambulant profound pupils enter our PMLD Drama Room. The room is dark and lit by fibre optics and a projected image of the sea. There are gentle sounds of the sea in the background. As they wait for the group to assemble staff concentrate on hand programmes, massage and finger decoration. The lesson begins and the book is introduced. Following an introductory song to gain attention and focus, the sensory objectives are delivered through simple symbols. A storyboard for the order of the book is created using pictures. The book begins on a mat depicting a boat. By using a Big Mack for 'more' the pupils make choices about weather conditions, wind (fan), rain (spray), sun (hairdryer). The pupils compete to gain control of the conditions. They interact with environments of shells, sand, mud, water and undergrowth. To depict the cockatoo a cloud of feathers is created (other materials can be used if asthma is a problem) and followed by a conversation of birdsong made by the pupils with the Sound Beam. In a tent the pupils controlled sound effects of jungles and explored trays of damp moss, fir cones and fluorescent spiders. Lastly they returned to the beach for a picnic where they were given appropriate support to exchange symbols for snacks. The story and objectives were finally revisited. After a few sessions the pupils began to anticipate aspects of the story and control the outcomes.

Note. The projected image was a screen saver of tropical fish swimming in the sea. The fish were 30 cm across and the pupils were able to interact with them.

Reading should be personalized

Reading trays can provide personalized programmes for literacy. Take note of pupil likes and dislikes and start from this point. Chloe likes brightly coloured things that sparkle. Harry likes buttons, switches and technological devices.

Chloe's reading tray Objectives: to communicate choices, reach, grasp and release objects	Rhyme – Pass the Treasure Chest Round
Glittered scarf Tinsel/baubles Large beads/shells Fluorescent rocks and feathers Crackly gold cellophane paper Smooth ceramic shards UV light	

Harry's reading tray Objectives: to recognize functional use of objects in a story and make correct choices to match the page	Book – *Freckles*
Book *Freckles* Electric toothbrush Water spray PECs cards Sponge/towel Sound effects on CD and CD player/headphones Tiny bed for Freckles	

Objectives must be personalized and steps must be kept very small. Activities need practice and repetition. Order and sequence must be maintained to ensure anticipation. Group work can be enhanced by the making of Multisensory Big Books and Story Sacks. Carefully chosen puppets which allow facial expressions and different mouth shapes can help focus attention and aid anticipation.

Music as literature

Music is a useful tool for providing access to literature. The patterns of language and poetry can be experienced through the singing of rhymes, songs and raps. This can be further enhanced through the use of a resonance board to focus on aspects of the language or the storyline. Such techniques can develop anticipation and memory. The teacher should play with words, sounds and rhythms by tapping on bodies, resonance boards, table, floor, drums or other percussion instruments and be guided by the pupils' responses whether they be silences, movements or sounds.

Reading is also about objects

Objects of reference

Objects convey information, and unknowingly form part of everyday communication. A child sees their lunch-box taken off the shelf and immediately knows it is lunch-time. No words have been spoken but from past experience the movement of the lunch-box tells him something about time, place and activities that will follow. Objects of reference can therefore be used to develop conceptual understanding for pupils with PMLD.

Objects of reference were originally developed in the Netherlands as a learning tool for a group of deafblind pupils but have been used increasingly to work with pupils with learning difficulties. At this level objects of reference have been used to develop experiential significance and, acting as an *aide-mémoire*, to give them the opportunity to understand and predict events within their environment.

In choosing objects of reference it is important to think of the contextual cues and the significance of the object to the pupil. It is preferable that the object itself be multisensory, e.g. be audible, be tactile and, where possible, include a smell. The giving of the object should include a rhythm or movement and have an interactive sequence with an adult. The use of a song or rhyme to reinforce the object is also effective.

Brent was always given the minibus keys before an educational visit. The keys were given as the song 'The wheels on the bus' was sung. The keys were jangled along with the song and handed to Brent. He quickly learned the significance of the keys and could lead the class to the bus. A confusing and anxious period of preparation became a relaxed and happy event.

Writing

Writing communicates sequences, stories, thoughts, events, experiences, information, emotions and feelings. Writing is a means of creative expression and helps us to store and retrieve ideas. It allows us to see ideas and gives structure and organization to thought processes. How can our pupils with profound and multiple learning difficulties be involved in writing activities?

♦ To develop hand control pupils need to bang, pat, poke, pluck, pinch, receive massages and experiment with tools and media to find preferences.

♦ To recognize patterns the pupil needs to experience sequences of patterns, use print rollers, make foot and hand prints, listen to rhythms of beats on resonance boards, explore ice-cube trays full of different colours and use lids and circular tools for printing.

♦ To improve story awareness symbols can be used to develop choice-making.

♦ To store and retrieve information pupils can use simple visual timetables using objects, photographs or symbols.

♦ To develop anticipation a teacher should provide well-told stories and rhymes, and use patterns of music and rhythms.

♦ To explore emotions use a Sound Beam, drums or a range of music. Look in mirrors and explore facial expressions.

♦ To develop eye control the use of tracking is essential using torches shone through balloons, candles and special lights. Linelite tubing, fluorescent patterns and objects under UV light provide an intense focus for eye contact.

Profound and Multiple Learning Difficulties

◆ To develop fine-motor and gross-motor skills use a range of doughs.

Cooked dough
2 cups of salt
4 cups of flour
8 tablespoons of cream of tartar
4 tablespoons of oil
Powder paint
4 cups of boiling water
Few drops of essential oil
Mix well in a saucepan
Then store in the fridge in an airtight container

Sawdust dough
5 cups of sawdust
1 heaped cup of wallpaper paste
4 cups of water
Mix well and store in fridge in an airtight container

Snow dough
4 cups of salt
1 cup of boiling water
Mix. Add 2 cups of cornflour
1 cup of cold water
Colour
Knead well

Baker's dough
4 cups of flour
1 cup of salt
1½ cups of water
Mix
Bake at 170C for one hour. Varnish

Cloud dough
1 cup corn/sunflower oil
6 cups of flour
1 cup of water
Food colouring and essential oil
Mix to bind
It S-T-R-E-T-CH-E-S

Ceramic salt dough
2 cups of salt
1 cup of cornflour
1½ cups of cold water
Mix in the top of a double boiler

♦ To develop tactile awareness and fine-motor skills develop hand-specific programmes:

Hand box programme

This programme is designed to exercise the hands and fingers and encourage pupils to reach into the space around them.

Each child has their own box of equipment, with each piece chosen to fit the size of the hand.

1. Sing 'Clap your hands and wriggle your fingers' (In and out the Dusty Bluebells). Encourage pupil to wriggle their fingers in the air

2. 'Stretch your hands and point your fingers'

3. 'Scratch your chin with all your fingers'

4. 'Touch your head and feel your hair'

5. Take each instrument in turn – tambourine for open palm, shaker for closed fist, squeaker for squeezing, buzzer or toy piano for pointing and pushing

At the end leave time to fill boxes while pupils choose favourite toy/instrument to explore independently.

Profound and Multiple Learning Difficulties

Hand programme			
Objective	Media	Attention/ eye contact/ timescale	Expression/ animation/ movement
Attend to hands	**Staff hands:** Under UV Fluorescent paint on hands Fluorescent gloves on hands Furry gloves, leather gloves, novelty gloves Faces on hands **Child's hands:** Fluorescent paint on hands Fluorescent gloves on hands Furry gloves, leather gloves, novelty gloves Faces on hands Cornflour paints		
Relaxed hands	Lavender in base oil as aromatherapy massage (parental permission needed)		
Attend to nails and fingertips	Nail varnish Fluorescent face paint		
Awareness of touch	Warm water/Cold water Porridge Paint White shredded paper under UV. Bubbles in water Jelly – hot, cold, set, runny, various colours Dough Fluorescent paint and cornflour mixed in large trays		
Attend to fingers	Bangles Rings, hair pompoms on fingers Finger puppets Finger cymbals		

Intensive social interaction – a model for working practice

Intensive social interaction focuses on what the child does or can do building his/her sounds and movements into communicative interactions. By treating these actions as meaningful the child will recognize they are communicative and have a shared meaning with the adult. These interactions become catalysts for future learning. Intensive social interaction should pervade all working practice.

Using the guidance established in the section 'The social environment' in Chapter 2 (pp. 28–31), the staff member should become tuned into the pupil. He/she should spend time watching in order to understand the movements and signals. Negative signals should be acknowledged as well as positive ones. They are both communicative. He/she should ensure adequate wait time is given and not be tempted to make things move forward. He/she should allow the pupil to take the lead. Responses should be selective. Too many responses will confuse and dominate the child

Initial indications that a pupil is aware may take the form of stilling, smiling, focused attentiveness, a rise in activity or vocalizations. This can be reinforced through imitation or mirroring. As an example: the adult imitates the child's hand movements, exaggerating the sounds made or tapping on the child's torso. This should not just mirror the movements of the child but also the quality of the sounds, including the force, tempo and rhythm of the sounds. The rhythm of the actions indicates the mood and emotions of the child and through the feedback the adult can demonstrate empathy and understanding.

As the child begins to recognize the interaction the build-up of dramatic tension is fun and can motivate the child to attend and concentrate. Build up this tension through vocalizations, slightly exaggerated movement and facial expressions. The child will begin to recognize the game being played. A child on a rocking horse will move his or her shoulders forward if the adult stops the horse. The adult dips his/her shoulders and sets the horse in motion again. The horse then stops and the adult waits. For some time the child's movement is a natural response to the loss of movement but gradually he/she becomes aware of the mirrored action of the adult who is waiting. The child exaggerates the movement as a signal to the adult and an interaction has been established.

The adult and child must work in close partnership so that the child sees that communication is a two-way process. Through the process of mirroring the adult creates a turn-taking experience which can be recognized and understood by the child.

Amy, a seven year old ambulant girl with PMLD and ASD (Autistic Spectrum Disorder) began to recognize that her actions in Soft Play were being mirrored by a teaching assistant. She enjoyed this new understanding. After some time another adult moved closer and Amy looked to see if she had the same effect with the new member of staff. She did and a whole new world opened up for her control.

The adult in this process needs to understand the importance of pauses as they may convey an important message, e.g. 'Your turn', or 'Do you want more?'

Elizabeth, a child with cerebral palsy, could recognize that her little splashes in a water bowl could establish better splashes by the adult. The pauses gave her time to say 'That's enough' or 'Do it again'.

Always remember in these sessions that careful positioning for comfort, eye contact and balance is important. Guidance from an OT or physiotherapist is worth seeking .

The aim of intensive social interaction is to develop intentionality. Intentionality is the child's understanding that a movement or action gains a reaction. The child learns that he or she can control things and make things happen. Gradually the experience of having these actions interpreted in this way enables the child to make them purposefully.

As the pupil builds a repertoire of communications through these activities his/her awareness develops; they begin to realize that they can now develop their own gestures, vocalizations and body movements to ask for what they want. It is important during this stage for the adult to remain interactive. Do not be tempted to replace the interactions with 'Well done'. In normal conversation this does not take place and it changes the relationship of the interaction. Do not be tempted to ask the child constantly for a sign or signal. This limits the child's choice and tells the child what to do.

Many children, as was the case with Amy, begin to reciprocate actions and initiate activities through imitations of your actions. As the child begins to understand the process, the adult can put more of her/himself into the game by changing the rhythm or sound of the action. The child will hopefully follow.

Some children do not want to interact. In these cases staff must demonstrate patience and flexibility, and always ensure that they are starting with the child's interest and not their own. They must remember it takes time to establish trust and a shared understanding. Persevere with the interactions without putting pressure on the child to conform. Look at the environment to ensure distractions are not hindering awareness.

Numeracy

When planning Numeracy programmes for PMLD students it can be initially frustrating if looking to the P levels for support and information since Levels 1–3 are generic and do not seem to draw out discrete curriculum strands to aid the teacher in understanding and planning.

The reason for this is that for those students functioning at these levels the key skills of Numeracy, Literacy and Communication are interrelated and overlap in many ways. It is, however, possible to plan programmes specific both to the student and to the subject of Numeracy and this section will endeavour to illustrate how best to do this.

What pupils with PMLD require in order to access Numeracy

Before planning the content of a Numeracy programme it is vital that the teacher has a clear picture of the student's prerequisites for learning – that is the student's individual learning style and pace, the need for reinforcement and repetition, motivations, sensory reactions and preferred learning environments. Staff should also consider factors affecting the pupil's emotional state:

- Is the pupil at home or in respite care?

- Is the pupil comfortable?

- Are the usual staff in place?

- Are the noise levels appropriate?

These are all factors that can have a significant impact on pupil learning.

Why is Numeracy important?

Numeracy for these learners will necessarily be based in early stages of child development and involve two important stages.

Personal exploration
From an early age babies explore their own body and develop an awareness of it in space and in relation to the world around it. As they grow older they experience objects that they can manipulate and explore with both mouth and hands. They begin to develop an early sense of number when holding first one, then two toys at the same time. They develop a sense of object permanence whereby they know that the toy just thrown out of their cot is still there. Through all these activities they are exploring concepts of Numeracy relating entirely to themselves and from these early explorations grows a need to communicate about their 'findings'.

Social interaction
Through the child's early exploration of the concrete world around it grows a realization of changes in that environment and consequentially a realization that the

child itself can affect its own changes in that environment. The child begins to engage in a cyclical pattern, described and named by Les Staves (2001) as 'The learning wave'. Individual exploration and experimentation leads to communication with others and an awareness of the other person's response. This response feeds back into the early ideas and concepts that the child is developing and effects changes through the new learning. This process repeats itself as the child continues to explore, communicate, receive feedback and adjust its understanding of the world.

These stages of development happen naturally and over a short period of time for most children. For the student with PMLD, however, there are multiple barriers in place which, without assistance, might mean that they never access even the earliest levels of exploration and therefore understanding and communication.

To gather information about the world around us we rely heavily on the senses of sight, touch, smell, hearing and taste and it is likely that the PMLD student has deprivation in one, if not more, of these areas.

To explore the world around us physically and independently we need control over our bodies and a perception of that control. Many of our PMLD students have physical difficulties which may prohibit this and the transference of information to the brain and its interpretation will be hindered by learning difficulties.

To communicate our experiences and receive feedback in order to learn we need an awareness of self and other and this is a stage which many of our students will not have reached, particularly those for whom Autistic Spectrum Disorder compounds their disabilities.

Activities relating to mathematical learning

As teachers we seek to aim high for our students and it can be very disconcerting when encountering our first student with PMLD and trying to plan for them. What it is key to remember is the stage of development that they are at and the deceptively simple skills that they need to acquire in order to build a relationship with the world around them. When we watch children developing at a normal rate we rarely consider the internalizing process that accompanies each game, each exploration and each manipulation of objects or toys. Yet this process of building internal pictures based on physical experience and of making connections through repeated experiences in a range of contexts with a range of materials is a crucial underpinning to all aspects of their learning and development. It is vital also to constantly remind ourselves of the huge limitations of access to the environment experienced by our students. Even the ambulant PMLD student is hindered from normal exploration by difficulties with motor skills and attention deficit among other barriers. Providing environments where the student is free to explore in their own time is crucial and even the placing of objects in an accessible manner for each individual student needs thought and planning.

It is possible to identify key concepts of numeracy for the PMLD student and to build these into a coherent scheme of work. Units of work can be planned to run alongside those for pupils working at higher levels or for a PMLD group working together on similar levels. In whatever setting you are working it is important to plan for a high level of repetition. Repetition both within the same setting then across a range of other environments and contexts is crucial for your student to internalize and process a skill or experience. How many times does the average two year old practise parking his car in the toy garage? Then fit a key into a door? a peg into a hole? a coin into a savings bank?

Key concepts for numeracy

Colour

Working on colour with PMLD students is very much about teaching them how to look. Although some students will have some form of visual impairment many of them will have no actual physical impairment of the 'equipment' needed to receive visual images and transport them to their brain. Low stimulation of parts of the body and brain can result in it ceasing to function properly so our job as teachers is to stimulate and help them to understand what they are seeing.

Multisensory environments and sensory hydro-pools are ideal for exploring colour. Colour-coded switches attached to bubble tubes and working with fluorescents under ultraviolet light are just two examples of highly visual and engaging colour activities. Flo Longhorn (2000) gives many more examples of activities in these kinds of environments. If you are not lucky enough to have access to such an environment in your setting there are other simple and inexpensive ways of creating good spaces to work in. A cloth over a table can make a working space for a small child. Tents are also very useful and can be improvised with a frame large enough to encompass a student and teacher. Even large golfing umbrellas can be used as a shared environment to shine coloured torches on and see the effects of light on different coloured and textured reflective paper.

Boxes of objects grouped by colour are a useful resource as are science safety goggles covered with different colour cellophane to experience how the world looks filtered through different colours. There are also many ICT resources freely available where choices about colour and contrasting colours can be used to stimulate vision. A good example of these can be found at the NGFL website under SEN Switcher (see Useful Addresses and Contacts section).

Patterns

Work on patterns with the PMLD student needs to be rooted in those which are fundamental to their every-day lives and environments and which help them learn to anticipate and be proactive within these patterns. Sequences of events, repetitions, patterns that are expected to finish but don't, relationships and greet-ings are all a part of this area of Numeracy. Turn-taking in activities such as rolling a ball or touching a switch to hear a preferred sound are good examples of building awareness of patterns. Using greeting songs until a sense of anticipation is reliably demonstrated and then stopping at an unpredicted point of the song will prove by response that the student is becoming aware of patterns. Smells, touches and objects of reference to indicate a change of activity are also useful in developing awareness of day to day routines.

Patterns can also be made with a variety of concrete, everyday items. Socks and shoes can be alternated, knives, forks and spoons arranged. Light sequences can be activated and then anticipated in sensory rooms.

An important aspect of understanding patterns for the student is their physical involvement with them. A simple dance routine in PE or the Expressive Arts which is cued by music or their given placement in a group of other students gives a sense of place and timing; as do songs that require active, if aided, participation to touch parts of the body or provide sound effects in a repetitive manner.

Counting

Counting is about finding numbers and understanding structure; in order to count a child needs to acquire certain skills. Normally, these skills would have begun to develop within the first few days of a child's life: responding to rhythms and sequences of daily events and even distinguishing between groups of different sizes. Learning the sequence of numbers comes before an understanding of 1:1 correspondence, knowing that each item being counted must have its own number. Pointing and using fingers to count, understanding the concepts of more and less and comparing groups of different sizes, all these skills have begun to develop by a developmental age of around two years.

For the PMLD student it is important that all counting sessions and activities are related to real-life situations and resources are therefore the things the student may recognize and use in their day to day experiences. Number songs and rhymes are useful, especially those relating to body parts and those to which concrete props can be added, and encourage the student to realize the fixed order of the number names. Work should focus on numbers up to five and begin with exploring the concept of '1'. Activities might include feeling one object, holding and stroking it, passing it from one hand to the other to feel that one hand is full while the other is empty, shaking a box with one object in to hear the sound it makes then reaching inside for it, pressing a switch to hear one interesting noise. It is important that all the activities physically engage the student in some way. The same activities will be appropriate for '2' and then '3', but do not move on too quickly. A planned session on the concept of '1' might be repeated weekly for a whole term and continue to stimulate the student and support their developing understanding. Look for other opportunities throughout the day to reinforce counting concepts such as counting the cups out for drinks or the number of pupils in a group. Use touch to identify each object to be counted and to encourage 1:1 correspondence. Net bags to hold single or groups of objects can be very useful aids for the student who has difficulties holding objects. They enable the student to experience the quantity by touch as well as visually.

Developing the concept of 'more' relies on watching closely for signals from the student. Using items or activities that it is known are liked by the student, begin the activity, pause, then wait for any sign from the student that they wish you to continue. Question 'more?' and continue.

Number
Number activities can be developed alongside counting and, again, the most useful activities for the learner

are ones using real objects in meaningful situations. Matching, sorting and sharing are key concepts of number and there are many practical tasks that are ideal for developing and practising these skills.

Matching is one-to-one grouping of items that are the same. Pairs of shoes, socks and gloves are ideal resources for activities. Beaded bracelets to match and wear one on each wrist and pairs of printed or photocopied hands and feet can also be used. Sorting is grouping into groups of like objects. Separating towels from swimming costumes following a hydrotherapy session, placing fruit in bowls for lunch, putting cutlery into separate boxes after lunch are examples of sorting. Sharing incorporates division and fractions since it is about parts of the whole. Food is an obvious focal point for activities since it is something we already regularly share. Cutting a cake or pizza into halves and quarters, dividing up an orange, pouring juice from a transparent jug into cups, dividing bread dough to make rolls are easy examples and there are many more that will spring to mind. Activities are not restricted to food; many classroom resources such as play dough will lend themselves to teaching this concept.

Cause and effect
Cause and effect is understanding the consequence of an action and therefore repeating it intentionally in order to repeat the consequence. Touch screens on PCs and interactive whiteboards have become invaluable resources for working on this area of learning, progressing to using switch-activated toys and programmes. Work on cause and effect involves choice-

making too. Choosing between operating a fan with a switch to get a cool breeze or a small fan heater or hair-dryer to warm up gives an important element of control to the student. Most electrical equipment can be linked to a switch and the range of activities possible is there-fore very wide. Microwaves to melt chocolate, bubble machines, lamps of all kinds and even popcorn machines can be built into programmes.

In a young child the development of an understand-ing of cause and effect appears to begin with dropping or throwing toys and watching what happens to them. Similar activities are appropriate here with the student as physically involved as possible. Knocking down towers of bricks and reaching for desired objects, learn-ing to pull a cloth to draw an object closer or move an object out of the way are all activities where the student is impacting on the environment while learning more about it.

Object permanence
The concept of object permanence is a very important one since it enables students to build fragments of recognition and understanding into a more complete picture of themselves and their environment. Object permanence is simply knowing an object still exists even if it cannot be seen. It is hard for us to imagine not realizing we still have hands if they are covered with gloves or not looking in the tin if we want a biscuit simply because by not seeing them we are unaware of their existence, but this is the case for many of our students who are at early stages in their development.

The development of object permanence requires the student first to have opportunities to explore objects with their hands, mouths or any part of the body in order to gather as much information as possible about size, shape, weight, texture, smell and temperature. They will also need chances to discover what they can do with it; what noises can be made with it? Does it roll away if thrown? Once this information is gathered you can conclude that the student will have some perception of the object and recognize that it is separate from them.

The second stage is for the student to realize that at whatever angle or in whatever context the object is presented to them it remains the same object and by handling other objects at the same time and in the same way they can increase its perceived identity by comparing qualities. Now that the student has a clear concept of the object, activities can be planned to gradually remove it from their sight. Half covering the object with a cloth is a good way to begin and as the student continues to reach for the object gradually covering more and more of it until it is completely hidden. As work progresses it is important to keep the range of activities as broad and as interesting as possible, using as wide a range of resources as you can and it is worth remembering that you do not need expensive, specially designed toys to work with PMLD students. Simple household items can be as effective as high-tech solutions. Take a look around your local supermarket and try to invent an activity for ten of the items you see on sale there!

Problem-solving
Problem-solving is using learned numeracy skills in an applied or practical way and at its simplest level can be

making choices in everyday situations whether it be choosing between juice and milk at drinks time or between two offered activities. The opportunity and ability to make such choices and to show likes and dislikes is empowering and is a really important aspect of numeracy for our students.

Problem-solving is also linked to cause and effect since it requires knowledge of the problem 'I want the dog to bark' in order to then project or remember the solution 'I need to press the switch'. This demonstrates an awareness of repeated actions and events that always have the same result.

A sense of time
The concept of time as hours and minutes is not one that the PMLD student will ever grasp. What can be taught, however, is an awareness of daily routines and a limited sense of history – what happened yesterday – and the future – what will happen tomorrow. A symbolic timetable using objects of reference to support meaning will inform the student about daily activities. Songs as introductions to each activity will aid transition between them and consistent signing will also support this and help the student to begin sequencing regular events and to be able to predict what will happen next. Sounds and smells are important clues to many students and it is useful to be aware of this not only in planning your objects of reference but in observing behaviour. Food smells coming from the kitchen may already indicate the approach of lunch-time and the sound of transport arriving inform the student that they will be going home soon.

Shape and space

Small children climb on, under and into things. They reach for things, roll things, squash, stretch and throw things. They look at things from all possible angles and positions and move their bodies in a huge variety of ways. This is how a child becomes aware of their body in relation to the environment and the qualities of the objects around them and when planning work on shape for our students we should aim to replicate as many of these experiences as possible.

Movement in water is sometimes the only time the PMLD student can move independently and choose for themselves where and when they will do so but other opportunities can be found for a change of movement to be experienced such as swings, hoists, soft play areas and cradling and sliding on mats and parachutes. As it is important for students to be aware of their bodies in space it is equally valuable for them to experience shapes in relation to their body. Being inside a box, under a table, enclosed by a sphere, rolled on a large physio ball help build an understanding of the world and the shapes within it. Mobiles made up from a range of everyday objects and changed regularly give opportunities to reach, hit and explore; and shapes of different sizes and textures are useful to explore from a range of angles and with different parts of the body.

Communication and Interactive Technologies

Although there is increasing use of computers for pupils with PMLD, information technologies need to be looked at in a much wider context than just computers. Pupils with PMLD use a wide range of equipment controlled by switches and this development has allowed increased autonomy and control of environments for these pupils.

Pupils with PMLD do not develop the ability to play in the usual ways. Furthermore the added help of instruction does not enable the learning of play to take place. However, if the sensory experience of objects and equipment is raised, e.g. with flashing lights, sound effects and attractive textures and movement, there is an increased likelihood of spontaneous interaction. Where the added complication of physical disabilities occurs, automated equipment helps to facilitate actions that occur consistently, e.g. the touch of a switch turns on a teddy that blows bubbles, or the touch of a switch activates the blender to make a drink. In developing these technologies it is always important to remember that not all equipment has to be high-tech, e.g. the use of a Neilson Little Room may provide consistent interactions from tiny movements made by a pupil.

Imagination has to be used by teachers to bring topics alive. The use of digital cameras to take pictures in learning situations can enable a pupil to begin to remember places and events if played back on screen at a later time. Create laminated photo albums of the pupils and those around them to interact with and share.

Switches

The most important areas of technology relate to the development of switching skills to aid communication and achieve environmental control.

Switches provide opportunities for pupils to understand the relationship between cause and effect and thus control their environment. Switches can utilize the smallest of movements and provide an excellent means of making choices, demonstrating preference, establishing anticipation, initiating actions and simple messages.

The disadvantage is the pupil needs to concentrate on two separate functions:

♦ the ability to control the switch

♦ the ability to watch or hear the effect

For many pupils this will take time to generalize.

Cause and effect

The most obvious example of cause and effect is the communication between two people. When we call a name we anticipate and expect to receive a response. Cause and effect is therefore not just about using switches to make things happen; it is about touching people and objects, prompting actions, exploration and investigation. The first time we experience cause and effect it may be touching the roughness of a Moses basket or an icy surface. For pupils with PMLD the learning process will be slow and require constant repetition to build up awareness, attention, anticipation and memory. Switches may provide a key.

Choice of switch

Factors affecting the choice of switch include its purpose, pupil control, lighting, and position.

It is important that the switch works reliably to enable the pupil to achieve success and confidence.

Message switch
These can be used as a simple switch or for the recording of sounds. Various types of these are available in a range of colours and sizes. Some companies make them as blocks of multiple switches.

Flat switches
These require less lifting power from pupils with very little motor control. They can produce very little sound and thus not enable the pupil to realize the switch has been activated.

Mat switch
These are useful to provide inclusive activities in technology. However, pressure requirements can make them problematic.

Sound switch
These are increasingly sensitive and can be used with very profound pupils, enabling sounds as small as the pupil's breathing to switch on fibre optics and bubble tubes.

Touch-stick switch
Two stick switches can be held together to operate technologies. These are useful for youngsters with cerebral palsy to control movements. One can be held by a supporting adult while the other is held by the pupil.

Movement switch
These can be very difficult to control. Other alternatives include devices controlled through the breaking of a beam such as Sound Beams.

Flat touch-pad switch
These are the simplest, cheapest and the most effective switch. Fluorescent or coloured.

Squeeze switch
These are activated by squeezing two wooden rods together.

Air switches
Now finding a place in multisensory pools. They are attached to beach-balls, air-beds, etc., with success.

Contact switch
These are activated by minute amounts of pressure. They are useful for pupils with little movement or poor control.

Pull switch
This switch is activated by pulling the rod that sits vertically on the switch.

Double-touch or grip switch
Both hands are required to grip or touch this switch.

Wobble switch
This has a long coiled spring with a coloured ball on the end. To activate the switch the ball is wobbled.

New switches are constantly coming onto the

market. It is worth working with a speech therapist or occupational therapist to ensure the most effective access technique is used. Check the robustness of the jack plugs as these can be weak parts especially when inserted in wall sockets where they can be leaned on or tugged.

Timing of switches

Switches may be used in conjunction with a range of timed programmes.

Timed devices
These are the most useful programmes and require a push to activate for a timed period and a second push to reactivate when the technology has switched off. They provide a more useful record of the understanding of cause and effect.

Momentary devices
To activate a momentary device the switch must be pressed and be held down if the effect is to continue. This is useful for pupils with cerebral palsy to control arm and hand movements. This programme also enables pupils that have understood basic cause and effect through timed switches to progress to the development of strategies.

Continuous devices
These are often linked to planned passive programmes that tend to be experiential rather than interactive but may be used for attention objectives and eye contact.

Press and release devices
These are less common but activate as the switch press is released.

Latching devices
A latched switch requires one press to activate and another to deactivate.

When introducing a programme to a learner you should choose the device that you feel is appropriate for your pupil and stick to it. It is important not to interfere with their learning process by constantly introducing new variables.

Positioning of the switch

The correct positioning of a switch is vital. It is important to develop a controlled movement which is reliable and which the student can repeat consistently and in comfort. This does not have to involve a hand. However, check with the physiotherapist that the movement you are encouraging is acceptable. The position will depend on the part of the body used and may require a universal switch mounting system.

The mounting system should provide reliable access so that it can be pressed with accuracy and intention. It may take time and involve a considerable period of trial and error to find the right system for access. Some hand-operated systems may require a sloping position to allow the hand to slip off after use. For pupils who press indiscriminately the switch may need to be positioned further away so that a reaching movement is necessary and a control is required to access it.

Seating

Seating positions are vital to maintain correct posture while allowing both interaction with the switch and the observation of effects. Try to ensure that the physiotherapist, speech therapist and occupational therapist are consulted. Again collaboration to ensure shared aims and ideas will minimize problems encountered and maintain consistency.

Computers

In addition there are many computer activities that can be of benefit. It is important that the computer fits in with the overall aims for the individual and does not result in isolation. Independence is an aim in itself and is not achieved by leaving a pupil alone at a computer for prolonged periods. Computers may be attached to touchscreens and switches but the pupil has to want to interact with them. The following are some examples of ICT for pupils with PMLD:

♦ The use of the Internet with switches or touchscreens. There are an increasing number of interactive sites for pupils with PMLD that can be used or downloaded.

♦ The use of CD-ROMs with touchscreens. There are myriad new CD-ROMs including sound, video and music files. Many encourage interaction or picture-building sequences.

♦ The use of free Internet downloads of music and video provide age-appropriate clips for teenage pupils to watch.

Profound and Multiple Learning Difficulties

♦ The use of touchscreen art programmes.

♦ The use of Photo album Power points about people and events that they know.

♦ The use of switch and touchscreen music programmes.

♦ The use of interactive software programs that build pictures, create events and produce attractive and attention-seeking effects.

Create clear, shared objectives that are focused on. Do not bombard the pupil with instructions and comments that do not relate to the original objective.

Progression with switches

Responses to switch	
Response	**Level**
Pupils show a reflex response to switch movement (blink)	P1(1)
Pupil startled by sudden noise of switch	P1(1)
Pupil allows physical prompts	P1(1)
Pupil stills to sound of switch	P1(1)
Pupil demonstrates awareness of hand or elbow on switch	P1(1)
Pupil recognizes familiar feel of switch	P1(11)
Pupil turns head to switch	P1(11)
Pupil turns head and eyes to sound source	P1(11)
Pupil able to watch prompted hand movements to switch	P1(11)
Pupil has eye contact with switch for a few seconds	P1(11)
Pupil watches adult's movements during a familiar switch activity	P2(1)
Pupil actively interacts with and explores switches	P2(1)
Pupil begins to request switch through gesture (reaching)	P2(1)
Pupil observes own actions with interest	P2(1)
Pupil remembers learned responses and presses repeatedly	P2(1)
Pupil anticipates switch use and familiar routines	P2(11)
Pupil can explore and interact with switches spontaneously	P2(11)
Pupil communicates choices of switch	P2(11)
Pupil uses trial and error	P2(11)
Pupil now links switch and effect	P2(11)

Profound and Multiple Learning Difficulties

Responses to effects	
Response	**Level**
Pupil shows a reflex response to effect, e.g. blink (light, sound, ICT)	P1(1)
Pupil startles to (light, sound, ICT)	P1(1)
Pupil allows physical prompts to effect (light, sound, ICT)	P1(1)
Pupil stills to effect (light, sound, ICT)	P1(1)
Pupil demonstrates momentary awareness of whereabouts of effect (light, sound, ICT)	P1(1)
Pupil shows pleasure in familiar effects	P1(11)
Pupil turns head to effect	P1(11)
Pupil turns head and eyes to sound/light source	P1(11)
Pupil able to track effect moving in horizontal or vertical line (light, sound, ICT)	P1(11)
Pupil attends intently to sounds and lights on the screen	P2(1)
Pupil reaches out to a touchscreen	P2(1)
Pupil turns to sounds and familiar routines	P2(1)
Pupil reaches to switch	P2(1)
Pupil focuses on effect for prolonged period	P2(1)
Pupil communicates preferences	P2(11)
Pupil looks for sounds and lights at appropriate moments	P2(11)
Pupil cooperates in shared explorations	P2(11)
Pupil shows consistent responses to pleasant and unpleasant responses	P2(11)
Pupil remembers effects and anticipates them	P2(11)

Responses to switch and effect	
Response	**Level**
Pupil requests switches and effects through gestures	P3(1)
Pupil reaches for switches out of reach and watches for effects	P3(1)
Pupil reaches for switch and repeats when timer switches effects off	P3(1)
Pupil observes the results of his/her actions with interest	P3(1)
Pupil begins to link time of hold to effects (momentary programme)	P3(1)
Pupil begins to control effects through his/her actions, e.g. pushing switches he/she likes but not ones he/she does not	P3(1)
Pupil shows clear choices (e.g. red or blue bubbles)	P3(1)
Pupil anticipates effects (light, sound, ICT)	P3(11)
Pupil builds pictures and stops after picture is built to watch effect	P3(11)
Pupil communicates choices of intent purposefully	P3(11
Pupil begins to look for switches out of sight to create effects	P3(11)
Pupil makes links of objects of reference (looks for switch on new device to turn on)	P3(11)
Pupil applies solutions to problems systematically, e.g. when it's dark, turn on a light	P3(11)
Pupil shows understanding of a range of switches and their effects	P3(11)
Pupil can watch an adult's actions and copy them to create an effect	P3(11)

Sex Education

The social inclusion agenda has raised questions about lifestyle and social experiences for pupils with PMLD. Today there is a greater recognition of their right to ordinary life experiences. These youngsters require opportunities to make friends and establish a variety of relationships which fulfil their social and emotional needs, but considerable challenges may be exerted on those who care for and teach them when these pupils expect a full sexual life.

The 1993 Education Act (section 241) required all schools to have a Sex Education Policy. However, where such policies exist they rarely give sufficient guidance in relation to pupils with profound and multiple learning difficulties. Professionals lack the confidence to provide a meaningful and appropriate sex education curriculum for these pupils. Staff need clear guidelines on issues of touch, sexual expression and masturbation and in establishing such guidance it is important to take a reflective approach. Staff must develop the ability to put themselves in the position of the pupil and think beyond the comfort zone of stereotyped responses and phrases. For sex education to be meaningful these pupils need to be allowed to make their own choices of friendships and relationships. These basic communication skills are the precursors of any meaningful sex education programme. From an early age pupils should be encouraged to demonstrate choices and preferences in a range of settings. This is the basis on which appropriate choices can be made later in life.

In the past the delivery of sex education has been sometimes delayed because of the fears of what lies ahead. This has meant that the essential developmental process is established and basic skills of choice-making and discrimination are learned too late. When pupils become sexually aware they are unable to make appropriate responses.

The partnership between parents and professionals is especially important. The professionals must respect the values of the parents with regards to sex education but take an important role in developing techniques. From as early as 10 years old it is worth establishing a dialogue for the future with regard to sexuality. Helping parents to work through their feelings about these value issues is important while respecting their final decisions about expectations of practice. Discussion of emotions will not be appropriate for these youngsters and therefore technique and appropriate behaviours may have to be taught in the same way as learning to use a switch or hold a spoon. The most basic sexuality skills that must be learnt are those of simple discrimination. These include knowing when and where to disrobe, masturbate, touch other people, and perform related behaviours. For most pupils this will be all they are able to achieve in the area of sex education.

Society is quite frightened about the sexuality of people with disabilities. As an example an individual may be unzipping his fly in preparation for the bathroom but be viewed by the public as exposing himself with very severe resulting ramifications. It is therefore important to socialize these potentially hazardous situations and work systematically on ensuring consistency of appropriate behaviours.

There are now a number of good schemes of work for sex education for pupils with SEN, some with excellent guidance for those with PMLD. However, in this area more than any other, the programme needs to be personalized to meet the individual needs of the pupils and to take account of the feelings of those persons closest to them.

5

Problem Behaviour and PMLD

A student with PMLD will often present with one or more behaviours which make working and development of the student difficult and may result in injury to both the adult working with the student and the student themselves. In identifying and describing the more common of these behaviours it is vital that we consider not only the possible causes but also see them as communications that can inform our work programmes and our planning. As in all aspects of working with pupils with PMLD the key to managing behaviours lies in our building an understanding of the individual, their signals and communications that are there for us to read if we work with care and sensitivity.

Violent behaviours

Common behaviours encountered are kicking, hitting, biting, pinching, scratching, pulling hair, pushing, butting, spitting and pulling at clothing. These may be directed at a fellow student but most usually at the adult engaging with the student themselves. An obvious aim is to reduce such behaviours since they can cause distress as well as injury but more importantly because they are likely to exclude the student from opportunities and activities that could aid their development.

Research has looked at various factors that may contribute to causing violent behaviour, including diet and noise levels. Certainly, for those students with heightened sensory sensitivity, noise and light levels and other sensory input can be very stressful and we will look more closely at this in the section on Autistic Spectrum Disorder. The two main causes, however, are as follows.

First, the violent behaviour may be a reaction to being encouraged to focus attention away from a pre-ferred activity in order to engage in a task that is not liked or understood. This transition can be made easier for the student by having a range of sung and visual clues to encourage them to anticipate the change in activity. Objects of reference such as a cup indicating drinks time or a wipe to smell indicating toileting reduce student anxiety and aid their transfer of atten-tion. A slowing down of pace and increased repetition of activities that the student is comfortable with within a work session may also need to be considered to reduce stress.

Secondly, the behaviour may be an act of frustration at not being able to communicate a want or need – the adult is therefore not providing or behaving in the way the student wants them to. The key to reducing these behaviours obviously lies in the adult learning to 'read' the student's signals as closely as possible and respond accordingly, developing more appropriate communications with the student.

In responding to violent behaviour it is important not

to see an attack as personal. These students have little, if any, control over their world and any 'communication' has value. It is useful to keep records of incidents that will allow you, over a period of time, to build up a picture of when and what the incidents are and then hopefully to have an idea of why they happen. With some students it is easy to see what triggers the behaviour, e.g. screaming and nipping whenever a specific member of staff approaches, but some students are much more complex in their responses and it takes patience and perseverance to understand their patterns of behaviour.

Self-injurious behaviour

The types of behaviour included under this heading are those where the student deliberately and repeatedly damages their own body. Behaviours include hitting or banging some parts of the body, biting, pinching, gouging with nails, tooth grinding and hair-pulling. These behaviours can be very distressing for those working with and alongside the student and also hold the danger of lasting damage and/or infection.

There are two main suggested causes for self-injurious behaviour, both, however, relating to self-stimulation:

1. That self-injurious behaviour is a reaction to pain in another part of the body and a way of dealing with that primary pain. Repeated injury causes the body to produce chemical substances similar to opium which give pleasant and calming sensations and ease the pain. This easing will reinforce the self-

injurious behaviour and the student will continue with it.

2. That self-injurious behaviour develops as a means of stimulation when the environment is deficient in sensory opportunities or when the student feels isolated.

On occasions physical intervention is used to prevent self-injury, such as arm splints to prevent facial gouging. Whenever physical intervention is used it is imperative that a Positive Handling Plan is written with the agreement and support of all agencies involved with the student, including the parents. This plan must state procedures and need for use and how often and for how long the restraint will be used. Other protective measures can also be taken such as cushioned helmets for those pupils who continually head-bang.

Medical possibilities must also be considered, especially if the incidence of the behaviour has noticeably increased, as it has been shown in research that students with ear infections or with tooth pain will increase the level and frequency of their self-injury.

For the adult working with the student, having ruled out medical causes, the main task is to identify other toys or activities which the student enjoys interacting with and, rather than respond negatively to the behaviours, respond positively when attention transfers from the behaviour to the new object. Indeed, it has been shown that focusing on the behaviour itself can cause an increase rather than a decrease in incidence. Depending on the individual student, toys that vibrate, smell interesting, have preferred textures or sounds have been successful in breaking the pattern of behaviour, as have massage and music.

Stereotyped behaviours

Stereotyped behaviours are those which seem to have no obvious purpose but which are repeated frequently, and sometimes continuously, in exactly the same manner. Common stereotyped behaviours in PMLD students include rocking the body backwards and forwards or from side to side, moving the head from side to side and fiddling with and 'twirling' a favourite object or own fingers usually close to the face.

In stereotyped behaviours or self-stimulatory behaviours the student derives pleasure from their behaviour. Stereotyped behaviours can increase at times of stress and, in some way, give a sense of comfort and reassurance. These behaviours have also been shown to increase when there is a lack of stimulation, indicating that the student uses their stereotyped behaviour to maintain an acceptable level of stimulation which creates for them a protective barrier between themselves and their environment.

Stereotyped or self-stimulatory behaviours can present barriers to teaching and learning as the student may use the behaviour to disengage with learning. There is also the question of social acceptability and inclusion. Many stereotyped behaviours look or sound odd to others and, even though our aims are for students to accept each other as individuals, such behaviours may discourage spontaneous peer interaction. The behaviours may also cause irritation or distress and prevent fellow students being able to focus on their own work and activities. It is therefore very important to assess the effect of each student's behaviours on both their learning and their learning environment before making a decision to intervene.

Behaviours associated with feeding difficulties

Rumination

Rumination is a term used to describe regurgitating food matter into the mouth and either chewing and re-swallowing it or allowing it to then run out of the mouth. This is quite a common behaviour among young people with PMLD and needs attention because of the detrimental effect it can have on the health of the student. Rumination can lead to dehydration, weight loss and malnutrition which can cause a range of medical problems, not the least important being to lower resistance to disease in students who are already often highly vulnerable. The food matter that is regurgitated has a high acidic content and this can cause damage to the teeth which in turn can induce toothache and painful gums. Pain and discomfort in the mouth can then lead to further feeding problems.

Studies into the causes and function of rumination suggest that one of the main reasons for it is the student's need for oral stimulation. In many institutions there are pressures of time and staffing at meal times and this can lead to hurried feeding of students with little emphasis on their engagement with the process. To discourage rumination it is useful to slow down the eating process and involve the student to the highest degree possible. Active participation can be encouraged at many levels, some examples of which would be waiting for a signal from the pupil before giving another spoonful and physically aiding the pupil to load their spoon with an appropriate amount of food and guiding it towards their mouth. Students should also be encouraged to take the food into their mouths themselves rather than having it 'emptied' in and sometimes massaging of the cheek and jaw can encourage chewing and swallowing. It has also been found that the consistency of foods can cause a higher incidence of rumination. Experiment with the solid content of meals in order to find the consistency which best suits the student. Once rumination has decreased, however, it may be important to gradually introduce a range of textures to maximize the opportunities for sensory input at meal times and to prevent the pupil growing to accept only one type of food.

Positive reinforcement of appropriate behaviour is very important and as you get to know the student better you will be able to identify the activities or sensory experiences that can be used as a reward. These could be access to a favourite toy, the playing of some music or an interaction with a member of staff. These experiences, as well as reinforcing the preferred behaviour, should also extend the stimulation that the student is receiving at a meal time and therefore positively impact on reducing the incidences of undesired behaviour. The cleaning of teeth after a meal has also been shown to have a positive effect for some pupils since, again, it extends the period of stimulation and also has the benefit of counteracting some of the oral problems associated with rumination.

Vomiting

Vomiting is similar to rumination in that food is brought back to the mouth from the stomach but by definition it is ejected instantly rather than being kept in the mouth or reswallowed. Vomiting tends to be either an attention-seeking behaviour or an indication of certain foods or textures not being tolerated. A simple log of food intake and incidence of the behaviour can often quite quickly show if it is the types of food or consistency which is causing the problem. If this is the case it is obviously sensible to spend some time offering only foods that can be tolerated in order to reduce the incidence of vomiting and when this is under control slowly introduce some variances to encourage the student to learn to tolerate a wider range of food experiences. Do not to let the diet become too predictable and try to vary textures and taste sensations as much as possible.

When vomiting appears to be an attention-seeking behaviour strategies as discussed for rumination are appropriate and it is also important to react as calmly and quietly as possible when it does occur, cleaning it away without comment. Praise and other positive reinforcements throughout the meal, on completing it and for a short time afterwards, coupled with reduced attention when the undesired behaviour does occur, will render the behaviour unsuccessful. If the student wants attention but does not get it for vomiting it is likely that the incidence of the behaviour will decrease.

Food refusal

Food refusal is quite simply when a student will not tolerate food in their mouth and, as well as spitting it out, will often fight, scream and become very distressed at any attempt to help them receive food. Some students with PMLD will suffer from tactile defensiveness which means that they have a heightened sensitivity to touch and this can extend to the areas in and around the mouth. Programmes of desensitization can be followed, extending across the curriculum, and these may lead to a gradual introduction of foods. Programmes are usually planned by a Speech Therapist and involve a progression of touch sensations such as stroking with a feather, brushing gently with a soft brush and encouraging the student to tolerate and explore a range of material sensations. Sometimes the situation and the threat to health is so severe that a student needs to be tube-fed to the stomach.

When refusal is linked to a preference for one type of food above another simple intervention programmes can be planned to encourage a broader intake of food. If milk in a bottle is all a student will accept, different flavours can gradually be added and then a move planned to introduce dairy-type puddings. If a student will only accept desserts, then strategies such as alternating spoonfuls of a savoury dish with that of a sweet one with appropriate verbal praise may be successful.

Medical issues

With all three feeding problems discussed above there may be underlying medical causes. Both rumination and vomiting can be caused not only by infections but by abnormalities in the intestinal tract where it joins the stomach. This is called gastroesophageal reflux and occurs mainly in students with cerebral palsy, as does abnormality of muscular function which may lead to food refusal. Food refusal may also be caused by abdominal discomfort and digestion problems. It is, however, often difficult to ascertain the real cause of an eating problem, to separate out medical issues from behaviour. Where there is a medical problem the behaviour may be reinforced by the attention the student receives. A student may vomit following or during a meal because of reflux, but find stimulating the process and attention of being cleaned up and learn to use the behaviour in the future to attract further attention. Similarly, a student with muscular difficulties may not attempt to eat foods in consistencies that they could learn to tolerate, and refuse and regurgitate where there is no medical need to do so.

Autistic Spectrum Disorder and PMLD

Autistic Spectrum Disorder (ASD) is considered to be a developmental disorder and is the title now used to cover what was previously described as Autism and Asperger's syndrome – initially described in the 1940s by Leo Kanner and Hans Asperger respectively.

The current, consistent view is that developed by Wing and Gould who described the three core aspects of Autism which are commonly known as the 'triad of impairments'. The impairments are:

1. impairment in social interaction

2. impairment of communication

3. impairment in flexible thinking

All three core aspects must be present to make a diagnosis of ASD, whatever the intellectual ability of the individual.

Students with ASD often also have heightened sensory sensitivities in one or more of the senses. They may not be able to cope with loud noise levels, rooms that have an echo, particular smells, certain tastes or textures in their mouths or on their skins. This makes for a very distinctive and specific 'fingerprint' for each individual with ASD, since they all, also, will have a specific profile of where they rest along the spectrum of each of the areas of impairment.

It is believed that a high proportion of students with PMLD also have ASD but, given the severe impairment of intellectual abilities and other compounding factors, very few will have been diagnosed and have it on their Statement. Parents of children of average or higher intellectual ability rarely notice any abnormality in their child's development till after the age of 12 months and often not before they have a second child to compare or their child enters pre-school settings where direct comparisons can be made. For the parent of a PMLD child there will be so many other concerns that ASD is often not considered as a contributing factor.

It is, however, important to those working with a PMLD student to consider the possibility of ASD because it can give insight into many of the behaviours and responses of that child and therefore inform our planning, approaches and strategies. The recognition of ASD in the PMLD student can lead to changes in their curriculum, focusing on teaching social responsiveness rather than on a skills-based curriculum. This can prevent possible complete withdrawal from social interaction and therefore enhance access to learning opportunities.

Impairment in social interaction

The PMLD student will already be functioning at a low level of interaction with others but the student who also has an ASD will present with an added lack of awareness of others and their feelings. As well as not responding to distress in others the student may not seek comfort when they themselves are distressed. As some ASD students do not experience pain and discomfort in the same way as others it is important with regard to their physical care not to rely on conventional communications of injury and infection to let you know something is wrong. An impairment in social interaction may also prevent the student from wishing to engage in play activities and they may quite forcefully reject approaches and attempts to interact with them.

Impairment of communication

Use of eye contact between the student and those working with them may be limited and may never occur at appropriate times. Patterns of facial expressions may not reflect those in other students and there may be a poor sense of personal space, e.g. getting too close to someone who interests them. Echolaic speech, repeating parts or the end part of what someone else has said, is common in more able students with ASD, but with the PMLD student this can present as a constant or regular repetition of a single sound or group of sounds. Some students also use this repeating of sounds to block out other noises that they find distressing.

Impairment in flexible thinking

A lack of flexible thinking means that the student relies on routines for comfort and a sense of control, and finds unexpected changes in their environment, staffing or activities highly stressful. Concrete objects may be fixated upon and become obsessions as they lessen anxiety and give the student this needed sense of control when other things around them are unpredictable and difficult to make sense of. Range of interests are therefore often limited since they must be activities or objects which can be relied on for their 'sameness'.

Sensory sensitivity

It is estimated that around 40 per cent of children with ASD have some form of sensory hypersensitivity. One or more senses may be affected, the most common being touch and sound, and the effect is of magnifying what would be ordinary sensations to the degree that they are frightening or painful to the child. It is possible that many behaviours described as problematic in the PMLD student will have been triggered or exacerbated by their hypersensitivity in one or more areas and it is for those staff who work with the student to explore these possibilities sensitively and endeavour to create working environments in which the student is relaxed and comfortable.

While working towards understanding a student where there are suspicions of hypersensitivity, it is important to be aware of the existence of synaesthesia. This is where a sensation experienced in one sensory system causes it also to be experienced in another. An example of this would be hearing different sounds whenever certain colours were seen. The physical reactions can be highly misleading to an observer, e.g. covering the eyes when a distressing sound is heard and it is therefore useful to experiment with a range of experiences to ascertain a correct diagnosis.

Sound sensitivity

Three main groups of sounds have been identified that commonly cause problems for students with ASD and sound sensitivity.

The first are sudden, unexpected noises such as a door banging, a shout or a balloon popping, sounds which may startle the average student but cause real distress for those with sound sensitivity.

The second types of sounds are those generated by many household and workplace machines. The high-pitched, continuous noise made by a vacuum cleaner, a washing machine or even a hand-dryer in a toilet can be all-consuming for the student with ASD. The amplification that is suffered can mean that a sound no one else is even aware of, such as the hum of a classroom heater, not only causes distress but obviates any other activity or focus of attention.

The third types are groups of sounds whose source and meaning the student is unable to ascertain and whose range of inputs is overwhelming. This is common in social situations where there will be a range of voices speaking over each other and perhaps music too. Shopping malls, swimming pools and other crowded places can also be very difficult experiences with their combinations of noises, voices and echoes.

It is impossible within a school environment to create working spaces where no sudden or machine noises can be guaranteed, but steps can be taken to reduce the possibilities of stress. Curtaining of large or echoey spaces can reduce noise levels as can the use of cork tiling on walls. Staff can be encouraged to move quietly and to move objects carefully when sharing a space with the student. Interruptions to working sessions should be discouraged. School assembly times should be accepted as potentially difficult and the student allowed either to wear earplugs or headphones playing preferred, calming music. These measures can be reduced as the student gains in confidence.

Tactile sensitivity

Tactile sensitivity can explain many behaviours in students with ASD since it underlies both positive and negative reactions to touch. Many students enjoy the sensations of certain fabrics or textures and will choose to stroke or scratch at them for periods of time. Some parts of the body may be more sensitive than others and it is often the case that light touches are less bearable than firm ones. Non-compliance with activities such as brushing hair and washing may often be connected with sensitivity as is the removal of clothes and fixation on certain items of clothes or outfits. Some students with ASD have heightened sensitivity on the palms of their hands which makes it difficult for them to join in a range of play activities.

Desensitization techniques can be used to improve the student's tolerance of touches they find difficult. These use a range of gradated brushing, stroking and massaging techniques to increase the time that touch is tolerated.

Using colours and activities that the student is known to like can be a positive way of encouraging them to feel a texture, e.g. provide sand, play dough or paint in their favourite colour, and latex gloves can be used as a successful barrier to help build tolerance and confidence.

If a student shows an adverse reaction to being stroked or hugged it may well be that it is the type of touch they cannot tolerate, not the connection with another person. Indeed, some students respond well to firm massage and holding and enjoy being rolled up in mats, rough and tumble play and using soft play facilities.

Visual sensitivity

Students with ASD often give the impression that they do not recognize or have an interest in an object or person because they prefer to use peripheral rather than central vision. This is linked with a tendency to focus on parts of objects or faces and a difficulty in absorbing the bigger picture of what they are looking at and the relationship between those different parts.

Such students also often have a strong fascination for particular types of objects, particularly those with repeating or rhythmic patterns such as wallpapers, streetlights, carpet patterns and the lines on roads. They also show particular interest in lights and shiny, reflective objects and may engage with them for long periods of time, often holding them close to the face.

Colours, brightness and complex design can cause a visual overload for the student to the point that they may retreat into stereotyped behaviours in an attempt to block the input.

It is not ideal to remove all visual stimuli from a classroom but useful if designated areas are created for working with the ASD student. If possible, work areas should have plain, neutral wall and floor coverings and overly bright light should be avoided. Work tasks should be laid out clearly on a contrasting background so that it is easy to differentiate them.

Food texture and taste

A student with ASD may well have difficulties with eating certain kinds of foods as well as with the way their food is presented. Smelling and handling food before eating is common as sometimes it is easier to identify the food by smell than it is by taste and it also reassures the student as to its identity before putting it into the mouth. A limited diet through fixations on certain foods is also common and it can be hard to introduce new tastes and textures. Building on preferences can be successful, however, by observing what is accepted readily and extending tolerance towards similar foods. For example, if a student eats raisins, a gradual introduction of other small pieces of dried fruit may extend the range of accepted foods. However, it is not usually a good idea to mix new foods with preferred ones to encourage a broader diet since foods mixed together generally, even fillings put onto bread to make sandwiches, can often cause distress to an ASD student. Similarly, it can be important to place foods separately on the plate at meal times rather than touching each other and not to cover with sauce or gravy unless an acceptance or liking for this has been ascertained first.

6

Support for Families

At the beginning of the twenty-first century we acknowledge that every citizen, including those with profound and multiple learning difficulties, should be valued and have equal opportunities for a good quality of life. This should include the families of those children who experience a quality of life devoid of many features we take for granted.

The government and concerned agencies know that we have a long way to go to establish a society in which everyone is equally valued and supported. This has to go further than creating laws and writing reports. Values and working practice have also got to change to ensure implementation in the future. Despite the strong voice of disabled groups in the implementation of change it is those who are most severely disabled who have been most neglected. The relationship between education and other services is still weak. Professionals find themselves bound by their roles and have difficulty marrying concept and practice. Stronger multidisciplinary collaboration is essential if the government's vision is to become a reality. As teachers we can play a part in developing that collaborative process. Schools are now creating a variety of forums for interdisciplinary discussion and working practice.

The range of care activities that parents now undertake is wide-ranging and would to appear daunting to most of us. Frequently their expertise outstrips that of service providers and becomes a limiting factor in support offered, e.g. a mother who now tube-feeds, gives suction or rectal diazepam may find respite care institutions unwilling to care for the child due to their own lack of training. Few mothers have their own full-time work and frequently employers are reluctant to employ a mother of a profoundly disabled child. Parents must become part of the multidisciplinary process.

Siblings of children with profound and multiple learning difficulties also need support. There are frequently restrictions on family time and activities, embarrassment in public, worries about bringing friends home and concerns for the future. As a teacher of a pupil with PMLD it is important that family considerations are planned for and the family are included in the process of planning

Respite care

Respite care is of great importance to the family with a child with PMLD. Sadly, the quality of this provision varies enormously depending on where the child lives and which authority is providing the service. Parents who have not discovered or taken up this service should be encouraged to do so to enable them to have a balance in their lives of family and care. Some parents are unaware of the respite services and need information and guidance. Others find it difficult to relinquish their child for respite because of fear or guilt.

Emotional support

Many families of pupils with PMLD need additional emotional support. Although some families rally around and develop their own mechanisms for supporting a family member, the loss of extended family relationships has left many couples unsupported and lonely. Meeting with other families in similar circumstances can be a vital lifeline for them. In other cases the strain of supporting a youngster with PMLD has led to separation, leaving a single parent working alone. The understanding of another family in the same position can bridge the gap for emotional support and understanding.

Many organisations such as Mencap, RNIB, Capability, Sense, ENABLE, the In Touch Trust and Contact a Family (CAF), have local branches who will provide this support. The CAF directory may also provide parents with useful information and contacts about specific conditions and syndromes. The In Touch Trust also produces a newsletter and publication with useful addresses and information.

Mencap's PMLD section PIMD has created a number of publications to help parents plan for the future.

PAMIS is an organization that provides a wealth of pamphlets and information for parents and carers of pupils with PMLD. Parents are involved in the planning and development of projects and workshops for PAMIS

Leisure support

Leisure time is seen increasingly as a gauge for quality of life and yet considerable barriers for disabled youngsters exist. Very often service providers are unaware of the law or the needs of pupils, some providers are volunteers and untrained. Helping parents to understand and access improved leisure time for their children is important. As teachers we should be ever-vigilant of opportunities for improving the life of these youngsters with whom we work, providing information and encouragement to parents.

Where possible we should extend the role of the school into areas of Study Support and after-hours activities to ensure the development of lifelong learning and a holistic approach to the child's care. Many schools now have Hydrotherapy Clubs, Healthy Living Clubs, Youth Clubs and a wide range of additional provision. Where pupils are integrated into mainstream schools it is important that areas of Study Support also extend to pupils with PMLD.

Transition to life beyond school

The education of pupils with PMLD is still evolving but it is generally accepted that it is in advance of adult care services. The process of transition can be cumbersome and confusing with complex Community Care Assessments and myriad new faces. The input from Connexions and Social Services and their guidance from the age of fourteen have helped to ensure that the process begins in good time. The future of a pupil can be planned well in advance to give time for families to think and assimilate information. This is a time when parents and carers need help and support to ensure that the needs of the pupil continue to be met.

The future

The wealth of new legislation has enabled people with PMLD to begin to take their rightful place in society as dignified and respected citizens. There is still a long way to go in ensuring provision and attitudes match the law. Parents need to be recognized as partners in the model and their needs as well as those of the child must be met. Improving the circumstances of the family can often be the most effective way of improving the life of the pupil with PMLD. This can only be achieved through a range of agencies, all of which need to work collaboratively to this end.

Appendix

Useful Addresses and Contacts

British Epilepsy Association
Freephone helpline: 0808 800 5050
International callers: +44 (0)113 210 8850
e-mail helpline: helpline@epilepsy.org.uk
Free fax helpline: 0808 800 5555
Epilepsy Action Head Office
New Anstey House
Gate Way Drive
Yeadon
Leeds LS19 7XY

British Institute of Learning Disabilities
Campion House
Green Street
Kidderminster
Worcestershire DY10 1JL
Tel: 01562 723010
Fax: 01562 723029
e-mail: enquiries@bild.org.uk

Cerebral Palsy Sport
11 Churchill Park
Colwick
Nottingham NG4 2HF
(video of adapted games)

Contact a Family
209–211 City Road
London EC1V 1JN
Tel: 020 7608 8700
Fax: 020 7608 8701
Helpline 0808 808 3555 or Textphone 0808 808 3556
Freephone for parents and families (Mon–Fri
    10am–4pm)
e-mail: info@cafamily.org.uk

Cystic Fibrosis Trust
11 London Road
Bromley
Kent BR1 1BY
Tel: 020 8464 7211

DfEE Parent Site,
http://www.parentcentre.gov.uk/

Disabled Living Foundation Advisory Service
380–384 Harrow Road
London W9 2HU
Tel: 020 7289 6111

Downs Syndrome Association
Langdon Down Centre
2a Langdon Park
Teddington TW11 9PS
Tel: 0845 230 0372
Fax: 0845 230 0373
e-mail: info@downs-syndrome.org.uk

The Drake Research Project
3 Ure Lodge
Ure Bank Terrace
Ripon
North Yorks HG4 1JG
(Music materials for pupils with learning difficulties)

The Fragile X Society
Rood End House
6 Stortford Road
Great Dunmow
Essex CM6 1H7
Tel: +44 (0)1371 875100

Interplay Theatre Company
Armly Ridge Road
Leeds LS1 23LE

In Touch Trust
Ann Worthington
10 Norman Road
Sale
Cheshire M33 3DF
Tel: 0161 905 2440
Fax: 0161 718 5787
e-mail: worthington@netscapeonline.co.uk

IPSEA (legal representation),England and Wales
Freephone: 0800 0184016
Scotland (ISEA): 0131 665 4396
Northern Ireland: 0232 705654

Kaleidoscope Theatre Company
19 Mellish Road
Wallsall
West Midlands WS4 2DQ
(Company of actors with learning disabilities)

Live Music Now
4 Lower Belgrave Steet
London SW1 W0LJ
Tel: 020 7730 2205
(Music for those too disabled to go to concerts)

Mencap
123 Golden Lane
London EC1Y 0RT
Tel: 020 7454 0454
Fax: 020 7696 5540
e-mail: information@mencap.org.uk

Profound and Multiple Learning Difficulties

NASEN (National Association for Special Educational
  Needs)
NASEN House
4/5 Amber Business Village
Amber Close
Amington
Tamworth B77 4RP
Tel: 01827 311500
Fax: 01827 313005
e-mail: welcome@nasen.org.uk

The National Autistic Society
393 City Road
London EC1V 1NG
Tel: +44 (0)20 7833 2299
Fax: +44 (0)20 7833 9666
e-mail: nas@nas.org.uk

National Deaf Association
Freephone helpline: 0808 800 8880 (voice and text)

Orcadia Creative Learning Centre
3 Windsor Place
Portobello Road
Edinburgh EH1 52A
(Arts courses and activities for pupils with disabilities)

PAMIS
Springfield House
15/16 Springfield
University of Dundee
Dundee DD1 4JE
Tel: 01382 345 154
e-mail: pamis@dundee.ac.uk

Rett Syndrome Association (RSAUK)
113 Friern Barnet Road
London N11 3EU
Tel (national): 0870 770 3266 (local): 020 8361 5161
Fax (national): 0870 770 3265 (local): 020 8368 6123
e-mail: info@rettsyndrome.org.uk

Riding for the Disabled Association
Avenue A
National Agricultural Centre
Kenilworth
Warwicks CV8 21Y

RNIB Holidays and Leisure Services
RNIB
224 Great Portland Street
London WIN 6AA
Tel: 020 7388 1266

Royal National Institute of the Blind
105 Judd Street
London WC1H 9NE
Tel: 020 7388 1266
Fax: 020 7388 2034

Profound and Multiple Learning Difficulties

Scope
Cerebral Palsy Helpline: 0808 800 333
(free and confidential advice, initial counselling and
    information)
weekdays, 9am–9pm
weekends, 2pm–6pm
e-mail: cphelpline@scope.org.uk

SHARE Music
15 Daremore Drive
Belfast BT9 5JQ
(Residential music and drama courses for pupils with
    learning difficulties)

SOUNDABOUT
12 Alfred Terraces
Chipping Norton
Oxon OX7 5HB

Soundbeam Project
10 Cornwallis Crescent
Bristol BS8 4PL

UK Sports Association for People with Learning
    Disabilities
Leroy House
436 Essex Road
London N1 3QP
Tel: 020 7354 1030

www.dundee.ac.uk/pamis/
www.jamesrennie.cumbria.sch.uk
www.ngfl.gov.uk
www.priorywoods.middlesborough.sch.uk

Bibliography

Aitken, S. and Buultjens, M. (1992) *Vision for Doing.* Edinburgh: Moray House Publications.

Baker, J. (1987) *Where the Forest Meets the Sea.* London: Walker Books.

Cheminais, R. (2003) *Closing the Inclusion Gap.* London: David Fulton.

Clark, S. (1991) *Children with Profound/Complex Physical and Learning Difficulties.* Stafford: NASEN.

Contact a Family (1991) *Siblings and Special Needs Fact Sheet.* London: Contact a Family.

Coupe, J., Barber, M. and Murphy, D. (1988) 'Affective Communication', *Communication before Speech*, ed. J. Coupe and J. Goldbart. London: David Fulton.

Davis, J. (2001) *A Sensory Approach to the Curriculum.* London: David Fulton.

Department for Education and Skills (2001) *Valuing People.* London: HMSO.

Department for Education and Skills (2003) *Every Child Matters.* London: HMSO.

Department for Education and Skills (2004) *Removing Barriers to Achievement.* Nottingham: DfES Publications.

Department of Education and Science (1985) *Curriculum Matters. The Curriculum from 5 to 16.* London: HMSO.

Hirstwood, R. and Gray, M. (1995) *Practical Guide to the Use of Multisensory Rooms.* TFH Special Needs.

Lacey, P. and Ouvry, C. (1998) *People with Profound and Multiple Learning Difficulties. A Collaborative Approach to Meeting Needs.* London: David Fulton.

Latham, C. and Miles, A. (1988) *Communication and Classroom Practice.* London: David Fulton.

Lee, M. and MacWilliam, L. (2002) *Learning Together.* London: RNIB.

Longhorn, F. (1988) *A Sensory Curriculum for Very Special People.* London: Souvenir Press.

Longhorn, F. (1993) *Prerequisites to Learning for Very Special People.* Wooton, Bedfordshire: Catalyst Education.

Longhorn, F. (1997) *Enhancing Education through the Use of Ultraviolet Light and Fluorescing Materials.* Wooton, Bedfordshire: Catalyst Education.

Longhorn, F. (2000) *Numeracy for Very Special People.* Wooton, Bedfordshire: Catalyst Education.

Longhorn, F. (2001) *Literacy for Very Special People.* Wooton, Bedfordshire: Catalyst Education.

NCC (1992) *The National Curriculum and Pupils with Severe Learning Difficulties.* York: NCC.

Nind, M. and Hewitt, D. (2001) *A Practical Guide to Intensive Interaction.* Kidderminster: The British Institute for Learning Disabilities.

Pagliano, P. (1999) *Multisensory Environments.* London: David Fulton.

Pagliano, P. (2001) *Using a Multisensory Environment.* London: David Fulton.

QCA (2001) *Planning, Teaching and Assessing the Curriculum for Pupils with Learning Difficulties.* London: QCA.

Bibliography

Staves, L. (2001) *Mathematics for Children with Severe and Profound Learning Difficulties*. London: David Fulton.

Worthington, A. (1996) *Useful Addresses for Special Needs*. Sale: In Touch Trust.